POWER
ABUSED,

POWER
HEALED

D1522247

PRAISE FOR
POWER ABUSED, POWER HEALED

"This is the best book on power and its abuse by therapists and spiritual leaders since Guggenbuhl-Craig's trenchant *Power in the Helping Professions*. Anyone whose therapy or discipleship has gone rotten through no fault of their own will find wisdom and comfort here. It should be required reading for all therapists and healers in training."

— Roger Woolger, Jungian analyst, regression therapist, noted international author and lecturer

"Intricate, many-layered, imaginative, based on real experience, engaging, moving, and thought-provoking, *Power Abused, Power Healed* is a many-faceted jewel, seemingly hewn from the author's own painful witnessing of the variety of misuses of power. Not only in her professional healing work as a psychotherapist and Spiritual Midwife, but also through digesting her own encounters of abuse at the hands of those in power, as well as her own temptations to perpetrate like misuses in turn, Judith Barr has lovingly polished by hand to rare luster the ordinary ore of life experience. The resulting gem moves me to bow in reverence.

"This is an important work, on a profound and timely subject, presented with humility, incisive insight, rich imagination and flashes of humor. I heartily recommend it — with the caveat, 'Reader, beware, for these stories work themselves into one's marrow.'"

— The Rev. Dr. Genia Pauli Haddon, psychotherapist and author of *Body Metaphors, Uniting Sex, Self & Spirit*, and *Through a Stroke of Luck*

"*Power Abused, Power Healed* is a needed tool for the bookshelf of every healer working today. How do we first heal ourselves in order to heal others? It is a burning question and one imperative to this age. Can we recognize when and if our own imperfections are surfacing in a session?

"This book, in a magical way, is gently powerful as it uncovers the types of abuse that can happen in our Spiritual Healing Communities. However unintentional abuses of power may be, even the most respected healers can fall prey or predator to their own imbalances.

"It was synchronicity when Judith sent me this book after I had just experienced abuse of power. The book literally picked me up out of my confusion and gave me clarity in Truth. I was able to step back and recognize the Emperor, the child, the tapestry weavers.

"Bless Judith for the timely delivery of her book. May it serve a great purpose for all, as it served a great purpose for my Self."

— Wendy Stevens, herbalist, founder of Garden Plum

"In her book *Power Abused, Power Healed,* Judith Barr's anthology of cases of abuse is comprehensive and relevant. It is a vision into one of the darkest aspects of human nature and offers a model for healing and even prevention. I found her writing style to be clear and accessible. Judith's commitment to the material is obviously heartfelt and I wish her the best in getting it out to the public."

— Laurie Layton Schapira, Jungian analyst and author
of *The Cassandra Complex: Living with Disbelief*

POWER
ABUSED,
POWER
HEALED

JUDITH BARR

POWER ABUSED, POWER HEALED
by Judith Barr

Mysteries of Life
Brookfield, CT
www.PowerAbusedPowerHealed.com

ISBN-13: 978-1-886264-24-3
ISBN-10: 1-886264-24-4

Cover Design: Ross Feldner
Book Design: L. Jeannette Feldner

Library of Congress Cataloging-in-Publication Data

Barr, Judith
Power Abused, Power Healed
by Judith Barr — 2nd Edition
Includes Glossary
ISBN-13: 978-1-886264-24-3
ISBN-10: 1-886264-24-4
1. Spiritual Life 2. Psychology 3. Power 4. Power Abuse
I. Title

Although our society is addicted to quick fixes, healing and transformation are not quick-fix processes. We are here not simply to heal but also to become conscious. This is a deep and sacred life task.

The stories in this book are composites of real life occurrences and give only the beginning steps in a person's healing journey, which unfolds for each of us according to our own unique life path.

The words *Spirit* and *the Divine* refer in this book to the essence of that for which people have many names, among them . . . God, Goddess, Jesus, Holy Spirit, Buddha, Allah, The Great Father, The Great Mother, Love and Truth, Nature, and The Life Force.

Again and again, I have experienced abuses of power
in what are supposed to be caring,
healing contexts and containers.
And, as is true at some level for us all,
what is done to us, we do to others.

So for both the sake of my own heart and soul
and for those I touch,
both personally and professionally,
it has been my life's work to heal this abuse of power
in my part of the world,
and to help heal it in the world at large.

With deep apologies to those I may have hurt
out of my own woundedness and unconsciousness,
and with expansive hope for the healing
of our use of power in the world,
I offer Power Abused, Power Healed
in service to this healing.

I pray what is in this book will not be misused or abused,
but rather will be used for the greatest good.

In Love and Truth,
Judith Barr

ACKNOWLEDGMENTS

I give thanks for the alchemical journey on which *Power Abused, Power Healed* has taken me. And for every single person who has come into the journey, for however long or short a time, however near or far away. It has all led to the birth of my book and so much more.

Everyone who has been a client or trainee with me has contributed to this process. Each participant in every workshop I have led has given to this book. Every therapist and spiritual counselor with whom I have worked or trained has added something unique. Each workshop I've attended or heard about has played a part. Every colleague with whom I've connected has provided something. *Power Abused, Power Healed* has been profoundly inspired by countless sources.

I call myself a Spiritual Midwife. And through the journey to create *Power Abused, Power Healed*, I have been blessed to have other midwives with me, each with the task of assisting in a unique part of the birth.

Corrie Triewth, thank you for being with me weekend after weekend as I first birthed each part of the book onto paper, then edited and re-edited the book. Through ease and strain, laughter and tears . . . at the very foundation of our long hours of work was rich joy. You were a god-send, a goddess-send.

Ren Haddon, your behind-the-scenes support and help were an indispensable, invaluable gift.

Sheila Levine, you have been like a Mama Lioness, looking out for my best interests, protecting me and my book every step of the way. I am so thankful.

Joyce Lynn, beyond gratitude for your skillful crafting of my book proposal and your tenacious editing, I am so thankful that you asked me to give the birthing push that reawakened my passion for the political and my joining the political and the psychospiritual — for the sake of my own soul's calling and for the sake of our world.

Cynthia Black, you have served the birthing of this book without even knowing it. It is astounding how one letter and one phone call can change a person's life and the path of a book.

Joel Roberts and Heidi Wall . . . There are times when we meet someone who truly sees us as we know, in our greatest vision, we can be. Both of you saw me, the work of my book, and the work of my calling. The journey hasn't been the same since. And Joel, your ongoing support, your sensitive truth-telling, your helping me think in terms I had only dreamed in my soul's longings, your patient, organic coaching, and the kindred quality to our interactions — all this and more. How blessed I have been!

Barbara Shine, you were a reliable, consistent presence helping me prepare the manuscript for printing.

Jeannette Feldner, in the journey to print you have worked your graphic magic, as you have done consistently for the past 15 years. For all these years, you have been a blessing in my calling and in my life. And Ross Feldner, thank you for every suggestion you made, every tip you gave, everything you did to help us in the process.

Holly Beyar, your steady assistance in every other aspect of my work has been key in making possible the unfolding of *Power Abused, Power Healed.* Your dedicated vision and input to the book's process have been crucial.

Dianne Disston, you have been such a magnificent midwife in this process — day by day, week by week, month by month, year by year. Skilled, constant, committed, trustworthy, real, and heartful. You have been a treasure. I couldn't have been more blessed.

Those in my personal life who have supported me in my journey with *Power Abused, Power Healed* and in my life as well, I give thanks for you every single day.

May everyone who has contributed to this book know that their contributions will have a deep and positive impact on me, on *Power Abused, Power Healed*, and on our world.

It is my prayer that all who come into contact with *Power Abused, Power Healed* will find that it is also, for them, a rich experience and so much more. May it be a source for deep, powerful transformation.

I give thanks for the Mystery of Life.

POWER ABUSED, POWER HEALED
THE DESIGN

My adaptation of Hans Christian Andersen's "The Emperor's New Clothes" forms the foundation for the stories and the teachings that follow. The price paid for the townspeople's burying their thoughts and feelings and silencing their children's voices, together with the necessary healing, make up the stories told in Chapters Three through Seventeen.

Each story opens with a different ending to the fairy tale and then answers the question, "What happens when a child is silenced?" Each story addresses a different psychological or spiritual abuse dilemma and its healing.

In the stories, children are abused by their parents and the community. Then abuse in their adult lives, often by pseudo-helpers or helpers in name only, evokes the old pain. The authentic healers in the stories have journeyed with their own painful feelings and know they may need to work with them again on a deeper level. As a result, they can help the injured adult heal the current and ancient wounds.

I begin the book with shorter accounts, first only the concept of the healing, and expand and deepen the healing in the stories as the book unfolds. This progression mirrors that of an individual's journey. Many years of experience have shown me that when people allow the flow of their feelings to take them deeper into their own unique journey, their feelings lead them home to the Divine.

A section called "Here and Now," which follows each chapter, offers the opportunity for each reader to personally explore the issues raised in that story.

CONTENTS

PROLOGUE

ower is like fire, lightning, wind, ocean — like life itself — a raw, vibrant force of nature. It has the potential for great harm and the possibility for magnificent good. Each of us chooses, whether consciously or unconsciously, how we will use the power of our own life energy.

Every form of power can be used well or misused.

The law has been used to manipulate as well as to serve justice. Parenthood has been used as a means of captivity, and it has been used to nourish a soul, helping it grow into fullness. Sexuality has been used as a weapon to rape and dominate, as a substitute for unmet childhood bonding and physical touch, and as an exquisite sacred expression of love and union.

Even God's name has been used both to destroy and to heal. Christian Inquisitors burned midwives at the stake; zealots have committed acts of violence all over the world in the name of religion. In contrast, people of many religions pray for peace; practitioners all over the world speak different names for God as they lay hands on suffering bodies to touch hearts and souls and restore them to health.

POWER ABUSED

Power is abused in every arena of life. Limitless instances of the misuse of power are hidden behind closed doors. Psychotherapists, massage therapists, and spiritual teachers violate their clients and students under the pretext of helping them heal and grow. Therapists pull rank in power struggles with clients. Massage therapists expose and touch clients unethically. Spiritual teachers elevate themselves so they can do what they wish with students, even if it goes against what they teach.

Many instances of power abuse make the headlines. One country invades another for its resources, under the guise of freeing its people. A national leader is bought by those who pay his bills, sacrificing the citizens of his country and the country itself. A corporation, looking after its bottom line, forfeits the environment for generations to come. Priests molest the children in their care and the church takes care of the priests. Young girls in sports are sexually abused by the men who coach them. An international celebrity murders his wife. A father rapes his daughter. A mother drowns her children.

We become blind to the cost of power abuse wherever it occurs: Our families, our institutions, our communities, our countries turn against others; and they turn against themselves in the same way a man with an autoimmune disease finds his own body turning against itself. We act as if these occurrences were normal, justifying them and, as a result, extending our blindness.

THE TRUTH ABOUT POWER

What a challenge it is for us to discern the real truth about how power is used!

Robert Karen, tracing the origins of misuse and abuse of power in his book, *The Forgiving Self: The Road from Resentment to Connection,* has written a clear, eloquent description of how this discernment can be reached:

"Power is another such tonic for wounded self love. To be able to control, to command, to be surrounded by eager supplicants and helpers also replicates the lost pleasures of infancy ....Our world is full of people who thrive on power and acclamation and feel empty and worthless without it. Is it any wonder that threats to power can, much like rejection, sexual betrayal, or public humiliation, engender an unforgiving rage of infantile proportions?

"Perhaps the most universal form of solace for the frailties we need to deny are the stories we tell ourselves about our lives. We soothe ourselves, consciously and unconsciously, with fairy tales tinged with grandiosity that leave us feeling less vulnerable than we really are. If you question my judgment, if you won't come when I need you, if you forget my birthday, if you raise your voice, if you don't love my dog, you may cause to collapse all the stories I've told myself about my own goodness; about the happiness, soundness, and security of my life; and about the control that I have over it. It all now seems a pack of cards. Once again, I inhabit the dark territory of depression and terrible truth, that area of unmourned loss, where I experience myself as hateful, unwanted, and alone. *And this is what I cannot forgive.* Indeed, this is why I hate you and want to kill you! To forgive you, I'm going to have to deal with the inner mess you've stirred up. In this realm of unmourned loss, forgiveness does not feel like an option. It is hostage to growth."[1]

Imagine! So many people in the world are hurting or killing others instead of dealing with their own inner mess. Imagine if all those people were to work through what's stirred up within them instead of creating a mess in the outer world.

---

[1] Robert Karen, Ph.D., *The Forgiving Self*, pp. 66-67, Doubleday, 2001.

POWER HEALED

As new modalities of growth and healing are birthed into our world, we need to be exquisitely careful. Many of these bodies of work do not train people in the intricate, complex workings of the psyche and soul. And they often are designed to create a quick fix, while avoiding deep, transformative explorations of feelings. Most people become intoxicated as they learn to use new theories and techniques. There is such a temptation and propensity to take that first drink and, finding how empowered we feel or how empowered we help someone else feel, become addicted. This addiction is fed by people's disconnection from their feelings.

We know ourselves and we know the Divine through our thoughts, our senses, our bodies, our prayers, and our feelings. Sadly, most of us were raised to believe we should cut off one or more of these pathways to the Divine. I have found the most commonly disconnected avenue is the feeling pathway.

Through my work, I hear from people about their deep fear of their feelings. When I broach the issue openly, clients can see how they defend against their feelings. Some use spiritual principles and spiritual paths — even affirmation and prayer — to circumvent their feelings and avoid going *through* the process to live from the Divine within.

What is needed for healing is a deeper, more feeling-based exploration and understanding of power abused and power healed. Aren and Mita, the healers in *Power Abused, Power Healed,* mirror my approach to working with feelings, incorporating aspects of my practice in their work.

I think of myself as a Spiritual Midwife, one who assists people in giving birth to their true selves and aligning with the Divine. I help them use their feelings as friends and divining rods to their deepest Self. I support people as they stop their repression, acting out, and sublimation of feelings. I teach them, instead, how to inhabit what they feel in a safe way that truly transforms their feelings into guides. Through this process, they develop the capacity to bear their own experience and to discern which feelings point to healing and which to right action.

Feelings are a bridge to the Divine; they help us align ourselves with the Divine. When we welcome and allow our feelings to flow safely through us, we welcome and allow the Divine in all its many forms of expression. The only way home to the Divine Self within is through our feelings. If we choose not to go through our original feelings, then the pain, in its distorted form, manifests as misused power or collusion in that misuse. In other words, *repressed feelings become power abused.*

As adults, we may be competent and function well, but we may also have a young child within us who is wounded, terribly frightened, and hiding beneath a confident front. When we can bring the frightened part into awareness, then we can truly heal and mature that child. Once we heal, we have the ability to help end abuse by speaking the truth and acting upon the truth — whether in a therapy room, a healing center, a family, a church, a community, a country.

Think of what our world would be like if the adults in the late 1930's and early 1940's had healed their wounds. How many Germans would have never become part of Hitler's defense force if they had done their work with their real fathers, if they weren't searching for an authority figure in place of an absent parent, or if they weren't re-enacting their experience with an abusive mother. Notice! The people Hitler gathered around him were a "defense force." The cruel, torturous, horrifying abuse of power Hitler created in Germany and all those he gathered round to help him was his way of *defending* against the repressed horror of his own childhood.

Alice Miller describes this in her landmark book *For Your Own Good: Hidden Cruelty in Child-Rearing and the Roots of Violence.* In her other books, including *Thou Shalt Not Be Aware: Society's Betrayal of the Child,* she tells us about abuse of children, the devastating extent of the problem, and the need for parents to do their own healing work.

Imagine if Adolf Hitler had done his own inner work! Imagine if he had healed the wounds of his childhood. The result: He wouldn't have dreamed of creating the devastation he did create; he would have used his charisma and his other gifts in service to humanity.

Claude Steiner, author of *The Other Side of Power*, offers the perspective that "it is possible to be powerful without abusing power, to be happy and alive and at the same time fair, considerate and cooperative." My explicit focus in *Power Abused, Power Healed* is on the worlds of therapy, recovery, personal growth, and spirituality. At the same time, there are windows and doors within every story that open out into other arenas of life. Steiner aptly put this focus in perspective: "The personal is political; our personal struggles follow the same patterns and motivations observed in local, regional, national, and global politics."

STORYTELLING

Through the vehicle of story, *Power Abused, Power Healed* can help us develop a mental and emotional discernment about power and can help those injured by harmful use of power to take a major step in their own healing.

The transformative power of story is part of history. Stories passed orally from generation to generation have held communities together, given people hope, inspired people in difficult times, offered people models to emulate. Bill Moyers honored this truth by creating a television series with Joseph Campbell, "The Power of Myth."

In ancient Jewish tradition, the Talmud guides the living of life and relationship with God through story. Jesus taught through parable. Stories from Buddhism can open a doorway to healing. Most of the world's faith traditions teach and comfort through story.

Story finds its way past the mind and through the defenses to the heart of the wound, touching directly but gently the pain that needs to be felt and worked through. Story offers multiple layers of gifts for healing and living.

THE RIGHT USE OF POWER

Power Abused, Power Healed addresses the right use of power by those in positions of authority in spiritual arenas, healing arts, politics and government, media, business, communities, and families, where the abuse of power is most hidden of all. In my field of psychotherapy, when emotional wounds need to be healed, they come into the open like the symptoms of physical illness. This is exactly what I see occurring in the world today. Symptoms of misuse of power — war, economic injustice, untrustworthy leaders and institutions — are in the open for everyone to see.

Similar symptoms of abuse of power are rampant in the healing arts right now. This abuse permeates psychological programs, spiritual paths, best-selling books, and television and radio programs, often led by celebrity hosts. Professional therapists and purported healers too often take seeds of gold and distort them into something abusive and destructive to themselves, to others, and also to their modality or path.

Power Abused, Power Healed is a call to consciousness for all who want to do the necessary soul-searching to help discern if we are in danger of misusing our power or of experiencing the abuse of power. It is a call to live fully, to explore the sacred mystery of life, to join the soul's co-creation with the Divine.

To answer this call we must acknowledge:

❖ We choose individually how we will use our power;
❖ We choose communally how we will use our power — as families, as neighborhoods, as towns, cities, states, countries, as a world;
❖ We *are* each part of the problem and part of its resolution.

In fact, in this stanza of his poem "Please Call Me by My True Names," spiritual leader Thich Nhat Hanh illustrates that we are each every side of the problem:

I am the twelve-year-old girl,
Refugee on a small boat,
Who throws herself into the ocean after being raped by a sea pirate,
And I am the pirate, my heart not yet capable of seeing and loving.

If we each take our share of the responsibility for the misuse and abuse of power — the problem and the solution — we are saying "yes" to healing our own wounds related to power. We are saying "yes" to healing the ways we have been wounded by someone else who misused his or her power with us. And we are saying "yes" to facing and healing in ourselves our abuse of power with others.

It is a daunting task. It calls us to dissolve our defenses and meet the pain beneath those defenses, the very pain that caused us to create them in the first place. It ignites a passion in us to give that task the high priority it inherently deserves. It leads us to answer in truth: When is a force used well and when is it misused? When is fire used in service to all, and when is it used for harm to some? When is lightning harnessed for well-being and when for ill? When is truth used as a sacred instrument and when as a tool of destruction? When is love used as a sacred river and when as a flow to manipulate what one wants to create?

The way I know to change the abuse of power is to commit to healing the misuse and abuse of power in my own life and then to help others do the same.

What is needed is to do the inner work, the work in the human psyche and soul, to heal, dissolve, and transform the roots of misuse and abuse of power and their consequences in the outer world.

My fervent longing is that *Power Abused, Power Healed* will prompt us, one by one, to make a commitment to the right use of power in our lives, and that commitment will have a cumulative healing effect on our systems and institutions and on our world.

IN THE BEGINNING...

FOR THE SAKE OF TRUTH

Once upon a time there was a little child. From the earliest age she wanted to help people.

One day, when the child was four, a lady came to the house and asked for money to help the sick children. The little girl ran to her sleeping quarters, got her savings pouch from under her mattress, brought it to the door, and handed it to the lady. She felt such delight that she could help those unfortunate children.

Time passed. The little child's family went to watch the slapstick comedy in the town square. She didn't like those performances. She felt sad for the person who was ridiculed or slapped around and mad that one person hurt the other. She couldn't understand why anyone would do that to another person, or why others found it funny.

She said right out loud, "I don't like this. One man shouldn't hurt the other." People in the square laughed at her and told her she was too serious and too sensitive and should go home and play child's games.

She didn't think there was anything she could do at the time, but she promised herself she would help change this in the world when she grew up.

Judy grew. She still didn't like it when people hurt each other. Sometimes she was hurt by other people. That was so painful! And sometimes she hurt somebody. It amazed her that what she did to others caused her just as much anguish as what was done to her. Even more.

In high school Judy was appointed to the Student Government Executive Committee. She went every day during her last class to take part in governing the school. She loved it. She loved the intricate workings of the school. She loved helping the students. She loved the power to accomplish wonderful things. She loved the recognition of a job well done — which was how she had come to be appointed to the Executive Committee two years in a row. And she loved the wisdom and kindness of Charlie, the Faculty Advisor to the committee.

Although she had no conscious idea what she would study in college, is it any wonder Judy ended up with political science as her major? Quite by an act of mystery! She had chosen a sociology course and knew within two classes that she would not be able to enjoy and learn from the professor who was teaching it. She had no idea what she would study instead, until the registrar offered her a sophomore class that still had openings — Modern Society. And her love affair with political science and government began.

A couple of months later, Judy was sitting in Modern Society class, alive with excitement about the day's lecture. Someone knocked on the door, summoned the professor, and they went into the hall for a few moments. When the professor re-entered the classroom, it was clear he had been crying. "President Kennedy has just been assassinated!" he told the students, tears streaming down his face. That was Judy's first conscious experience of abuse of power and its consequences, even though she couldn't have named it at the time.

Some years later, still passionate about government and politics, she began to volunteer in political campaigns, supporting candidates in whom she believed and trusting the impact of each person's contribution. As a result of her work, a candidate asked Judy to be her campaign manager for city council. She accepted, honored and scared, admitting she knew nothing about running a campaign. Though the candidate said she would teach Judy, no real help was given, and relentless backbiting surrounded the campaign. Without warning or explanation, Judy was asked to leave. Hurt and disillusioned, she left, deciding that politics and government were not the right paths of service for her after all.

This was her second conscious experience of abuse of power, even though she still couldn't have named it at the time.

In the early 1970's, no longer a part of the political/governmental scene, Judy was heartbroken and once again disillusioned by the Watergate scandal, Richard Nixon's dishonesty, and the duplicity of those in high places in his government. Watergate broke the final thread of her desire to serve through government and opened a doorway, which would lead her to her true calling and path of service in the world.

This was her third experience of abuse of power, and this time she *could* have named it if she'd been asked.

Years passed. Judy went into a personal and spiritual emergence that led her into group therapy. She was *fascinated* by the work. She loved the intricate workings of a person's mind, heart, cells, and soul, including her own. But even more important, her life began to change from the inside out. She began moving, as if taken from a very linear, conceptual, rational way of living into an ocean of feelings. At times she descended slowly. At times she dove in despite her fear, even in spite of herself. Sometimes it seemed she was being pulled from below. And at other times, she felt like she was drowning. One minute she was totally in the dark. The next she had a clear sense of what was going on in the larger picture. Who knew that this time of healing, growth, and transformation would help her become who she was really meant to be, both personally and professionally?

The therapist and group members kept sharing with her that she had a real gift with people. She decided to train to become a therapist. And now began her passion for depth psychotherapy and grounded spiritual healing. She was thrilled by the teachings: *What lies unknown and unresolved in an individual's unconscious, drives and creates conditions that are different from what he would wish to create in his life and in our world.*

She could not have articulated then what she felt deep within — maybe there's abuse in politics and government but never in psychotherapy and healing. Therapy was where healing was supposed to take place! This disillusionment would be even more difficult and painful than the one with government and politics.

She began to witness people being abused in workshops, therapy and training groups she attended. Not all of them, but far too many. When she was aware of what was occurring, she stood up for those who were being abused. She experienced abuse herself in some of those contexts. She heard stories about therapeutic and spiritual abuse from her own clients. She was distressed by what was evident.

Judy worked with these events in her sessions, in her heart and in her soul. She needed to for her own life's journey. And she knew to really serve others she needed to do her own work with power. A veil was lifted. Memories of people abusing their power in her own childhood emerged. Recollections, both subtle and overt, of people in her family, friends' parents, teachers, clergy people, even shoppers in stores came flooding forth.

The disillusionment brought pain. It always does. Since we hold onto our illusions to defend ourselves against pain, when the illusion is stripped away, it lays bare the pain it was holding at bay. The disillusionment also revealed the places where she was tempted to or actually had misused her power. This brought even more anguish than the times when she had witnessed or suffered personally from another's abuse of power.

But the disillusionment also brought clarity and truth and a fierce, yet loving, determination. Judy utilized each memory, each current experience to help her become a better therapist and spiritual counselor, to help her use her power well. She took her training and her own natural gift and created a way of doing her life's work that she intended would help her prevent misuse and abuse of power in her practice. After many years, much experience, development of her own maturity and wisdom, and transformation from Judy into Judith, finally she came to the place where she had to help not only in her own sacred work with people, but also in the world outside the walls of her office!

She continued by writing an article in one of her newsletters, "For the Sake of Truth Itself." In it she began to expose the truth: There are healers and teachers who misuse and abuse their positions of authority and some of the principles in their fields, causing harm to their clients and students as well as to themselves. The centerpiece of the article was a powerful retelling of the fairy tale "The Emperor's New Clothes." It came flowing through her as she opened herself to inspiration. She had always loved the idea of the child who had the courage to speak the truth! She had always felt a kinship with that child.

Once the article was out in the world, once she had said to the universe, "I am willing to see and feel, and I long to help," more and more examples of the abuse of power in the healing professions came into her view. She became aware of them through clients and colleagues and experiencing them firsthand in numerous arenas — the workshop circuit, radio, television, books, and videotapes.

Millions of people were being affected. They didn't seem to realize they were being abused. This was heart-boggling to Judith. Her clients would tell her that through their work with her, they became aware of the damage a workshop leader, an author, or a radio therapist was doing.

"Roarrrrrrr! I *have* to do something to help stop this!" The Mama Lioness within her came to life and was compelled to take steps: to help people become aware; to assist people in protecting themselves; to help people prevent their own misuse of power.

And so this book, which had, itself, been for many years longing to come to life, was conceived.

I was the little girl. I was Judy. I am the Judith in this story.
I am the therapist and spiritual helper.
Just like every other human being on this earth,
I have had to work with my own wounds,
resulting from others' misuse and abuse of their power.
Just like everyone else, I have had to work with the places in me
that would be tempted to misuse and abuse my own power.
I continue to do this work because I know it is crucial
and because I can do no other.
It is part of my commitment to myself,
to my clients, to Love and Truth, and to this world.
And I am the Mama Lioness,
committed to help heal the misuse and abuse of power
within each of us, amongst us, and all around us.
I am the Mama Lioness who has written this book,
Power Abused, Power Healed.
It begins with the retelling of the fairy tale…

ONCE UPON A TIME . . .

THE EMPEROR HAS NOTHING ON AT ALL

There once was an Emperor of an ancient country. So taken was he by appearances that he could attend to nothing and no one else. Anyone who remotely threatened his appearance or his attention to his appearance was in grave danger. But his subjects knew this, so they had all learned to adapt in order to protect themselves. They hid their thoughts and feelings from themselves and everyone else and prayed no one would ever find them out.

One day, two seemingly fine men came to the castle and, through their own skill at appearances, passed themselves off as royal weavers, capable of weaving a cloth so fine that clothes sewn from it would have the special quality of being invisible to anyone who was not fit for office or who was extraordinarily flawed in character.

This appealed to the Emperor, who decided he had to have a garment of this cloth for the sheer purpose of discovering who was fit and who was flawed. As all the empire heard about the cloth, the people also got caught up in finding out which of their neighbors were fit and which were flawed.

So the two pretended weavers set up two real looms and asked for the finest silk and gold threads. They stashed away the threads for themselves, while play-acting at weaving the cloth on the empty looms.

After a few days, the Emperor became curious. Hesitant to go himself to be first to see the work of the weavers, he began sending some of his most trusted advisors ahead of him. One by one the advisors went to the *weaving room and were stunned to find that they were unable to see the cloth. Each one, afraid of what it revealed about her character or his fitness for office, kept the truth a secret, and instead made a grand appearance of appreciation for the weavers' fabric. And each one reported to the Emperor about the beauty of the cloth, which the phony weavers had described in great detail.*

When finally the Emperor was brave enough to go see for himself, the cloth had already been sewn into fine garments. Although he found himself unable to see the clothes, fearing for his office and the reputation of his character, he pretended to see them. The pretense of all involved multiplied and multiplied, as the Emperor was asked to remove his clothing and put on the new clothes for the procession that was about to occur outside the castle. He, like everyone else, pretended every minute detail, including admiring himself in the mirror.

And as he entered the courtyard and the streets of his capital, all the townspeople also made a great pretense about the clothes, each one fearing for the discovery of his flawed character or the loss of her office.

Finally, a block away from the castle, a little child's voice was heard saying, "But the Emperor has nothing on at all!" The child's father responded, "Listen to the voice of innocence!" The child's mother responded, "You are so brave, my child, to say the truth when everyone else is silent!" And what the child had said was whispered from one person to another. Until at last all the people were heard saying, "But the Emperor has nothing on at all!"

And although the Emperor and all his attendants knew the people were right, they felt compelled to take greater pains than ever to uphold the pretense.

HERE AND NOW

CHAPTER TWO
THE EMPEROR HAS NOTHING ON AT ALL

Most people I've met or worked with have at some time in their lives thought or even said, "The Emperor has nothing on at all." Perhaps they have seen through the pretense of someone like the wolf in the fairy tale, "Little Red Riding Hood." Maybe they have not been fooled by the seduction of someone like the old woman in the folk story, "Hansel and Gretel." Possibly they have not been deceived by the parent who says, "This is for your own good," as a justification for a spanking. Or perchance they have not been tricked by an alcoholic mother who claims to be celebrating her family as she drinks her third scotch on the rocks.

Reflect backwards through your life and find an instance when you were like the little child who wanted to say out loud, "But the Emperor has nothing on at all." What happened if you actually said it aloud?

POWER ABUSED,
POWER HEALED...

WHAT YOU FEEL CAN HURT YOU!

Finally, a block away from the castle, a little child's voice was heard saying, "But the Emperor has nothing on at all!" The child's father, physician to the Emperor, whispered in her ear, "It's all right, sweetheart, I'll take care of you. Nothing matters except that I love you." He gave her kisses all over her face.

When she said, "Stop, Daddy!" he responded by kissing her all over her delicate little torso. She laughed and laughed, in spite of herself, attempting to tell him "no" all the while. She called out for her mother, who had already turned away and occupied herself with the Emperor's garments. As he promised to always take good care of her and to love her forever, the child's father kissed her on the mouth, scooped her up into his arms, and carried her home. The little girl, who trusted her father completely, went with him, yet felt frightened, very excited, and confused.

Once home, the little girl's father lay her across the bed and touched her and kissed her all over. Although he kept telling her how much he loved her and how precious she was to him, the little girl twisted and tried to wriggle away from him. Finally, her father said she was a bad girl for not wanting his love. And as he walked away, he told her she would be sorry she made him not love her anymore.

Rachel grew up. She no longer remembered the day the Emperor had nothing on at all. She walked through her life yearning to trust people. But again and again she re-experienced her trust betrayed by men who said they loved her, would take care of her, and had her best interest at heart. Being a minister herself, she naturally went to a spiritual therapist to find the root of her difficulty and heal it.

What a kind man Bob seemed! Assistant Director of an up-and-coming metaphysical therapy institute, he committed to getting to know her safely and sacredly. To Rachel, his status and his commitment were signs of good things to come. He was not afraid when she felt and expressed the feelings that lay within her. She'd never experienced that before. Most people, she had found, were afraid of feelings. He appreciated her strengths and gifts, but also her vulnerability and realness. He welcomed both the little baby and the wise woman aspects of her. Rachel was amazed and touched by his wisdom and empathy. In fact, after a period of developing trust, she bonded with him, as a baby would with a mother.

Bob had a suite of offices at the institute. The outermost room was a waiting room, sometimes used as a group therapy room. Then there was a consultation room in which he worked with individual clients. There were two doors off the back of the consultation room. One was a bathroom. The second always remained closed and had a sign saying "private" hanging on it. This room was for Bob's own personal use between sessions.

Shortly after the bonding occurred, Rachel came for her appointment, only to find the usual consultation room was being remodeled. Bob came out of the room she had never before seen and gestured her through the door. He apologized for the cot that was in the corner and explained he was sleeping there because he was in the process of a divorce.

To her horror, there surged within Rachel a romantic feeling toward this man that had never before existed. Yearning to heal thoroughly, she, of course, told him of her feelings. Her instinct said they had to do with her childhood, probably her relationship with her father; but she didn't understand the connection. She didn't want to have these feelings toward this man, who, oddly enough, had become her spiritual mother. Rachel worked with Bob to heal both the current experience and the ancient roots.

She felt frightened, confused, yet very excited. In spite of herself, these feelings toward her counselor were very pleasurable. She knew she shouldn't have a relationship with him now, while he was her therapist; but she wondered if it might be right to have such a relationship once she had completed this process. She had known a number of people, colleagues included, who had fallen in love with and married their therapists.

Rachel asked Bob how he felt about her and if they might ever have a romantic relationship. She knew her young self needed him to say, "I have a love for you like a parent for a child; I would never betray that love to have a romantic relationship with you. It wouldn't be good for you. It wouldn't serve your soul." But that is not what he said. He told her, "I won't have a romantic relationship with you now, but I can't say that I never would."

He left the door open — which both excited and terrified her. She was flooded with conflicting responses. She was a tangle of questions. Could she still trust him? Was he still safe? Did this mean she had to take care of her own safety in the meantime? Should she be grateful that he was at least being honest with her? Did his truthful answer mean he *was* safe? Was it her responsibility alone to deal with this?

She told him honestly of her feelings, her fears, her frightening dreams of the beginnings of sexual contact with him. She asked for his help to heal this stirred-up-scary experience within her. She learned this jumble of feelings was called "erotic transference." And she discovered that when you are in transference with another person in your current life, you are unconsciously transferring onto that person feelings and atti-tudes that you originally had in relation to important people in your early life — like parents, grandparents, siblings.

Bob didn't call Rachel "bad," he didn't make fun of or belittle her, and he didn't tell her to keep it to herself. He encouraged her to relate to him every intimate and erotic detail. She hoped such confession would assist the process of healing and transforming these feelings for him, which were titillating and at the same time made her very uncomfortable.

So afraid was she of these feelings and what might happen between them, that she transferred her amorous feelings onto one man after another. Without being conscious of it, she began dating each one of them in order to keep her relationship with her therapist safe. There were difficulties in these relationships, both emotionally and sexually; and she took every intimate interaction to her therapist, who again listened intently.

After hearing a great many of these confessions over a long period, Bob could not contain his reaction to her erotic accounts any longer. One day in the middle of a session, Bob leaned forward and almost whispered to Rachel, "You know, Rachel, my dear, after all this intimate work we have done together, I am realizing that I have felt romantic and sexual feelings for you all along — even from the time you were first bonding with me and right up to this very day."

She was shocked! She had thought she had been healing all this time with a safe spiritual therapist. Now she felt otherwise. And yet she still wanted to tell all that was in her heart! She wanted to talk about it and to understand what this really meant.

She knew instinctively about secrets: that keeping secrets is a theft, meant to create an outcome that could not be achieved if the secret were revealed; that keeping secrets spreads poison in the underground labyrinths within and between people. She wanted to know how Bob's secret feelings for her all this time had affected both their work and her life.

Bob would not talk about that, but instead insisted, "It's all right, Rachel. Nothing matters except that you are very precious to me. I have taken care of you and I know you so well. You are more at the heart of my life than I ever realized until now, fearing that you will stop working with me because of my feelings for you."

This expression of his feelings excited her. She hadn't known how much she meant to him. It was like a dream come true to have him cherish her; but what she really wanted was for him to cherish her as a mother would her daughter. She was confused. Each time she attempted to talk about this, he tried to distract her by asserting his loving feelings for her.

Week after week, despite his efforts to sidetrack her, Rachel wouldn't be swayed from seeking to know and understand the full truth about what had happened in their therapeutic relationship and its impact on her life.

Unable to meet the demands of the situation, in the middle of a session, Bob pushed back his chair, stood up, put his hands on his hips, and stared at her with piercing eyes. He declared, "Rachel, it's about time you just forgave me for loving you and put this to bed. It's obvious you refuse to do that, and as a result, you are alienating me beyond measure. I can work with you no longer. This is our last session."

He escorted a distraught Rachel out of the office, closed the door firmly after her, and insisted he would never have contact with her again.

As the door closed behind her, Rachel felt as though Bob's big hands, hands she had once loved, were pushing her down the hall, into the elevator, and through the parking garage to her car. Once behind the wheel, Rachel was beside herself. This experience felt so familiar, yet she couldn't figure out why. Instead of driving home, she went to the house of her loyal colleague in ministry, Mita.

A wise and grounded minister, Mita listened with compassion as Rachel confided the whole story. Rachel told how her spiritual therapist had said he was ashamed of his feelings and so had told no one about them — not his own therapist, not his supervisor — but instead had pushed them down, attempting to squelch them.

And Mita explained that we cannot get rid of our feelings by pushing them down. In fact, as much as we may wish, we cannot banish our feelings at all. They remain inside us until we bring them out purposefully and consciously to work through them, resolving them, healing them, transforming them back into their pure essence — life energy.

Mita helped Rachel realize that even though her therapist's romantic and sexual feelings were under the surface and not acted upon, they were having a profound effect on Rachel all along. It was likely *his* romantic feelings, like a magnet, had drawn out Rachel's feelings for him. In fact, his hidden, un-owned romantic and sexual feelings for her had held them both captive all this time.

Rachel felt the truth of Mita's words. She felt relieved, she felt liberated; but at the same time, she felt shocked and angry at Bob's role. She had thought it was her problem, but all the time he had really been using her for his own purposes. He had been enjoying her expressions of love for him and his feelings of love for her and had been titillated repeatedly by the intimate details he had encouraged her to share, regardless of how doing so harmed her.

How could she not have known? How could she have been so blind?

Mita assured Rachel that in the spiritual therapeutic relationship, just as in the parental relationship, the doctor-patient relationship, or the teacher-student relationship, it was the caregiver's responsibility to prevent such a thing from happening. She told Rachel, "When one is called to be a professional caregiver, one needs a radical commitment to living responsibly — not only in one's actions, but in one's thoughts, feelings, and energies, as well. This doesn't mean professionals are any more perfect than parents. None of us is perfect. But when we choose to become a therapist, a doctor, a teacher, a healer, a pastor, we need to heal our wounds. We need to heal not only for our own sake, but so that out of our unhealed wounds, we don't cause harm to others. And when we do cause damage from our woundedness, we, as helpers, need to take utter responsibility to heal with the one we have hurt."

Rachel broke in, "It was bad enough that he hurt me, but worst of all, he didn't own up to it."

"Out of our wounds, we hurt others," Mita continued, "and more often than not, people do not accept responsibility, but rather blame the damage they cause on someone else. Hopefully, humankind is in the process of developing the true, undistorted ability to take responsibility. Eventually, parents will take responsibility for the ways in which they hurt their children. Friends will take responsibility with each other. Teachers will take responsibility with students — employers with employees, lovers with their mates, and nations with nations."

Over the course of several intense weekly meetings, Mita helped Rachel understand that her therapist had been acting out of his wounds, keeping his feelings secret, and blaming Rachel for his inability to face himself. She also taught Rachel that her own vulnerability to what happened must have come from her personal history.

And Mita helped Rachel trace the familiarity of the experience and feelings. Again and again, they trusted Rachel's feelings to be divining rods leading to their origins. In her own organic rhythm and time, from a place of real safety, Rachel found herself back in the Emperor's town.

The first memory: Standing a block away from the castle, her young voice innocently piercing the chatter in the square, "But the Emperor has nothing on at all." The second memory: Her daddy whispering, "I love you," and kissing her all over her face.

Finally, Rachel cried out, "I thought he loved me!" Then she followed the river of her sobs to the scene on the bed where she wriggled away from him and he scolded her, "You'll be sorry you made me stop loving you."

This time, with Mita present, Rachel was able to come through it with new consciousness and new life. Mita helped Rachel comprehend that her experience with Bob was a reenactment of her experience with her father. The awareness and the release of feelings opened a door to life energy that had long been buried within.

HERE AND NOW

CHAPTER THREE
WHAT YOU FEEL CAN HURT YOU!

Review . . .

A spiritual therapist breaches a sacred trust and harms someone he is treating.

Rachel's father molested her when she was a child.

As a young woman and adult, Rachel found that men, even though they said they loved her, betrayed that trust. At a metaphysical institute, her therapist, Bob, acting out of his own wounds, developed romantic and sexual feelings for Rachel, but blamed Rachel for pursuing the truth.

Rachel knew that keeping secrets creates poison in the underground labyrinths of our souls. Mita, a colleague and a wise, grounded minister, helped Rachel see that adults molested as children are especially vulnerable to abuse when they grow up. Mita helped Rachel heal from Bob's abuse and use her feelings as divining rods to connect to the origins — her father's abuse.

Consider . . .

The relationship with a spiritual counselor, the therapeutic relationship, or the relationship with any personal helper is a sacred trust. When a person chooses to become this kind of helper, he or she is saying "yes" to assisting another soul on its journey on every level of being — physical, mental, emotional, energetic, and spiritual. Sadly, not everyone who accepts the role of helper understands or follows through on this charge.

❖ What experiences have you had with the sacredness of such a relationship being breached?

❖ What personal experiences have you had with such a relationship being held and lived as sacred?

And Then . . .

Although pleased with her new understandings and her newfound ability to follow her feelings to their origins, Rachel was hungry for more. Because Mita was her colleague, it wasn't appropriate for her to continue helping Rachel with her healing. She referred Rachel to a trusted friend, who was a spiritual therapist herself, and Rachel continued the process of healing herself and the complex consequences of her experience with her father.

TRUST ME

Finally, a block away from the castle, a little child's voice was heard saying, "But the Emperor has nothing on at all!" The child's father snorted, "What do you know?" The child turned to her mother. Even her mother mocked her, "Little miss know-it-all!" The child's aunt challenged, "How'd you ever get such a crazy idea into your head?" The child's neighbor taunted, "If you think you're so smart, prove it!"

The child responded, "Well, I just walked up to the Emperor and touched his undergarments, and I could feel that he has no clothes on."

"But," the mother replied, "these clothes are invisible to anyone who has something wrong with them. So if you don't see them, something's wrong with you."

"But I'm not just talking about not seeing them, Mama. I'm talking about proving they don't exist by touching and feeling what does exist."

"Silly child," said the father. "If you can't see them, you can't feel them." The aunt added, "Ignorant child. She's got rocks for brains." The neighbor chimed in, "Simple child. I never heard such a foolish thing."

The child stood there stunned and confused. Why couldn't anyone else see something that seemed so clear and obvious to her? Maybe she really didn't understand. Maybe there was something wrong with her after all.

Rosemary grew up. She no longer remembered the day the Emperor had nothing on at all. She lived life as earnestly and lovingly as she could. But she kept having experiences in which people demeaned her for what she knew to be true, in ways that seriously breached her trust in them and her trust in herself as well.

For some years, she had repeatedly experienced her husband belittling and hurting her. She didn't know what to do with her pain or how to repair the relationship. Any time she tried, he hurt her again. She bought book after book and attended many seminars, trying to solve this problem. She didn't trust her husband and felt she should be able to resolve her mistrust. She was convinced she had to find a way to forgive him and to just love him more. She had been deeply hurt by him, over and over, yet had begun to think the problem might be all of her own making.

One day, hoping to get some help, she went to a public workshop. It had the fervor in the air of a religious revival. Hundreds and hundreds of people came from all over the world to work with a famous couple — a psychiatrist husband and his spiritual healer wife — Ralph and Celestial Young.

Ralph asked for volunteers and, in desperation, Rosemary went up on the stage. She allowed him to attach a microphone to her collar and then innocently, and earnestly, told him of her dilemma.

While Celestial looked on, Ralph began interacting with Rosemary. "You have been deeply hurt by your husband, haven't you, Rosemary? You've tried and tried, turned yourself inside out, and there has been no repair between you, has there? You want so much to resolve this with him, don't you?"

Although he didn't give her time to answer his questions, she felt they conveyed an understanding of her pain and a kindness for which she was grateful. She relaxed into the exchange between them.

Then he told her abruptly, "But the truth is, Rosemary, if you don't trust your husband, it's because you have trust issues. Maybe your parents hurt you, and you developed a defense of not trusting anybody. Maybe your parents undermined your trust in yourself when you saw things clearly and they denied them. I'd lay odds that you wouldn't know who is trustworthy and who isn't. I'll bet you don't trust me. But it's not about me. Everyone else here trusts me. It's about you and your trust issues."

Celestial added, "Do you see what Ralph's saying, Rosemary? If we expand it to its greatest dimensions, he would say that you wouldn't even trust God. You're so scared that your husband's going to hurt you, but it's your lack of trust that is causing that to happen."

Rosemary was surprised Celestial did not acknowledge what she herself had noticed: Ralph had baited her, pretending to be loving, and then switched into harshly demeaning and blaming her.

Rosemary was stunned. She was also confused and scared. She didn't believe what Ralph had said. It didn't feel true. But she didn't know how to prove it. And why did Celestial reinforce it? Probably because she was his wife. Why did the audience seem to believe it? Why didn't anybody seem to be able to see through what this man was saying? But maybe she didn't understand at all. Maybe there was something really wrong with her after all.

To avoid public humiliation, Rosemary lied to Celestial and said she did see.

In the ladies' room after the workshop, Rosemary was crying. Something about this scene felt really familiar and very painful.

Another woman approached her and introduced herself as Mita. She handed Rosemary her card and said, "Please call me. I believe I can help you with this. I am a spiritual counselor. I attended the workshop today because I have been terribly concerned about what is being taught on the workshop circuit and about the manner in which it is being taught. I decided to come in person, so I could have a better sense of what I may do next to help and protect people just like you, Rosemary. Will you call me and make a time for us to talk. . . no charge? Just because you deserve the truth and the help to heal from this, and just because I want to do that for you and for our world."

Rosemary was touched by Mita's presence and by her offer. She called the next morning and Mita invited her to come in that afternoon.

As their time together began, Rosemary heard and felt Mita's positive intention. They went over what had happened during the workshop.

And then Mita continued, "Ralph was cruel to you, and you do not deserve that. And rather than stop his meanness, Celestial supported it. My heart breaks for you. I am filled with sorrow, Rosemary, that you were treated that way at all, but also that you were treated that way in public."

Rosemary wept from the pain of how Ralph and Celestial had been with her and with joy and relief for Mita's response.

"And my heart breaks, Rosemary, for all those who were watching and either experienced the pain as they saw Ralph abuse you or, even worse, took in Ralph and Celestial as models for how to treat others. My heart aches over the participants who silenced themselves rather than take the risk that Ralph might treat them the way he treated you. My heart hurts so for our world as more and more people start to abuse one another in the name of growth and healing and spiritual truth!"

The power of Mita's words brought a fresh flood of Rosemary's tears. Handing her a box of tissues, Mita continued. "I also want to talk with you about trust, Rosemary. What Ralph taught you and hundreds of people from all around the world yesterday *was not true*!

"Trust is a complex concept. We all need to discern what is trust-worthy and what is not. This discernment applies to ourselves as well as to others. I may trust myself, or believe I do, and actually be trusting an aspect of myself that would mislead me. Or I may truly trust myself and be able to tell what's trustworthy and what's not.

"If you don't trust somebody, it may mean you have trust issues and it may not. You may be afraid to trust anyone as a result of early experiences. Or you may truly experience someone's untrustworthiness and have the wisdom to trust your own instinct.

"If you're the only person in a group who doesn't trust someone, it may mean your trust Geiger counter is broken; it may mean the other group members' trust detectors are malfunctioning; or perhaps some people have detected what's going on but you are the only one brave enough to speak out. There are many possibilities. So, Rosemary, as I said before, trust is a complex concept. And when you add to the concept the experience of the heart, the complexity grows."

As Mita spoke, Rosemary felt more and more ease in her body. Mita could see this change and continued. "It is true that if your parents hurt you, Rosemary, damaging your trust in them, then you probably did create a defense in the form of resistance to trusting. How broad that resistance became would depend on, among many things, your experience of trust with others in your life. For example, if your parents weren't trustworthy but your grandmother was, that would increase your ability to trust.

"At one point in your life, that defense may have been a very good protection for your psyche and even your life. But now, Rosemary, this kind of defense, paradoxically, will draw the very people to you who aren't trustworthy. Or, with this kind of defense, you might draw trustworthy people to you, but you may see them through the distorted glasses of your defense and be blinded to their trustworthiness.

"To sum it up, Rosemary, I know of some spiritual traditions that teach similar distortions about trust. Such teachings can be dangerous, undermining a person's clarity and true instinct." Mita took a deep breath and then continued. "Just like we need to know where other people are trustworthy and where they are not, so also we need to know where we, ourselves, are trustworthy and where we are not. Then, we need to commit to heal the untrustworthy places within us. It takes a lot of work of the psyche and spirit to be able to do this."

"Ah," sighed Rosemary. "It is a great relief to have you confirm what I know to be true. During the workshop, I felt all alone and unable to prove the truth. I believe Ralph had it set up so it would be impossible for me to address his abuse. He even said, 'I'll bet you don't trust me. But it's not about me. Everyone else here trusts me.' If I had tried to confront his untrustworthiness, he could just make it about me. It felt like I couldn't win with him."

"I think you are right, Rosemary," returned Mita. "Perhaps you were wise to stay silent this time, since the kind of deceit he was practicing is insidious. I have seen it happen too frequently in healing and spiritual work. The argument made seems true or is correct in form but is actually invalid. People get hooked by the appearance or the form. This is a very subtle brand of deception."

"Mita," said Rosemary, "I didn't stay silent because I was wise, but because I was stunned and confused in a very familiar way."

"Oh, I see," answered Mita, "I'm glad you are aware of that. When have you experienced that before?"

Rosemary shared a number of adult and even late-adolescent experiences that felt similar. Her husband had been tender and loving during their courtship; after their wedding he had begun mocking her. Her college boyfriend had pursued her with romance and gentleness until after she made love with him the first time; then he began to slowly pull away from her, slinging denigrating remarks at each step back. Her best friend had been a kind, compassionate confidante ever since they were thirteen; with no warning at all, she had humiliated Rosemary publicly several months ago.

Then Mita asked, "What was your very first experience of that nature."

Rosemary could not remember. Mita asked if Rosemary would like to try an experiment in an effort to find the first time, utilize it for healing, and so prevent future experiences of the same sort from affecting her in the same way. Rosemary gratefully jumped at the opportunity.

Mita suggested that Rosemary close her eyes and inside herself be back at the workshop, feeling exactly the feelings she felt at the time. She said, "Rosemary, imagine you are sitting at the top of a sliding board, feeling those feelings. And now you let yourself slide down the sliding board to the very first time you felt the same thing."

Rosemary surrendered to the process and slid down the sliding board. When she landed, she found herself a block from the castle, saying,

"But the Emperor has nothing on at all!" And she heard her father say mockingly, "What do you know?" She heard her mother sneer, "Little miss know-it-all!" She heard her aunt belittle her, "How'd you ever get such a crazy idea into your head?" And she heard the neighbor ridicule her, "If you think you're so smart, prove it!"

She felt all the same feelings she had felt during the workshop. But this first time, because she felt so young and vulnerable, the feelings were very intense. In addition to feeling stunned and confused, Rosemary began to feel her humiliation, her fear, and finally her rage at being treated that way and having her trust in herself and others so deeply undermined. She and Mita both allowed and welcomed wave after wave of feeling, staying present until the waves subsided and Rosemary opened her eyes, bringing back with her the vibrancy and self-trust that she had lost the day the Emperor had nothing on at all.

HERE AND NOW

CHAPTER FOUR
TRUST ME

Review . . .

Celebrity "healers" misuse therapeutic principles about trust, harming not only the person in the spotlight but also the followers who look to them for guidance and model behavior.

As a child, Rosemary discerned the truth by touching and feeling what existed, but her parents berated her into silence. She grew up and had experiences in which people seriously breached her trust in them and threatened her trust in herself.

At a public workshop with the air of a religious revival — led by a famous couple, Ralph, a psychiatrist, and Celestial, a spiritual healer — Rosemary went on stage for help with trust issues with her husband. Ralph baited and blamed Rosemary, while Celestial looked on, reinforcing her husband's stance.

Later, Mita, a spiritual counselor, gave voice to the pain healers can cause. She told Rosemary, "My heart hurts so for our world as more and more people start to abuse one another in the name of growth and healing and spiritual truth."

Consider . . .

We all have places where we are conscious and trustworthy and also places where impulses that are beneath the surface of our awareness lead us to be untrustworthy. We need to live with integrity in our conscious lives, but we are even more trustworthy when we commit to meeting and working through the hidden untrustworthy places as they come to our attention.

The story of Rosemary happens again and again in various arenas of our world today. Participants and witnesses who blindly believe leaders like Ralph and Celestial are similar to the townspeople in the fairy tale. Actually, blind trust is natural in a young child; but in an adult blind trust precludes discernment, tainting a person's trustworthiness.

Exploring trustworthiness is delicate and challenging but crucial in our development.

❖ Have you fallen for phony weavers?

❖ Mentally scan through your life and find places where you have been trustworthy in both big and little ways.

❖ Recall instances when you have not been trustworthy.

❖ Reflect on times when others in your life have been trustworthy.

And Then . . .

Before Rosemary left Mita's office, they talked about options for "what's next." Rosemary was comfortable with the results of her appointment with Mita and decided she would simply enjoy her new vibrancy and self-trust. It was, after all, why she had gone to the workshop in the first place.

YOU ARE RESPONSIBLE
FOR EVERYTHING

Finally, a block away from the castle, a little child's voice was heard saying, "But the Emperor has nothing on at all!" The child's mother pulled him back against her body and clamped both of her hands over his mouth. The father nonchalantly put one arm around his wife's waist, the other hand pushing against his wife's two hands.

The little boy looked up at his parents wide-eyed. He saw them gritting their teeth. He saw their eyes were flashing fire. He thought, 'Oh my God! They hate me!' He went limp against his mother. Their silencing had succeeded.

Sam grew up. He no longer remembered the day the Emperor had nothing on at all. He was always afraid inside. He appeared to function well in his life, so no one else could see his fear. And the appearance sometimes fooled even Sam himself.

Underneath his seeming competence were tell-tale signs within: Sam could not see clearly the dynamics going on around him in his family, at his job, at his place of worship, in any kind of group; and he was unable to speak when his input about things was needed.

After a particularly painful experience of this kind at work, Sam could no longer deny his need for help. He got a referral from a friend for a spiritual advisor, and the very next week began to work with Aren, whom Sam found to be kind, gentle, and honest. He began to bond with

Aren and to trust him immensely. With this as a foundation, Sam's mask began to thin, crack, and dissolve, laying bare his terror. For over two years he and Aren worked with nightmare after nightmare, moving the fear through his body and revealing clues to its ancient beginnings.

Sam grew so much with Aren's help that he decided to participate in a week-long group workshop run by a well-known leader. He went with the intention of giving his best, both to his own healing and transformation and to supporting that of his co-participants. But as the workshop unfolded, Sam became inexplicably uneasy in his body. He watched. He listened. He sensed. He felt. He felt worse and worse as the workshop continued. Something was happening that wasn't right, but nobody else seemed to see it, sense it, feel it.

The leader was blaming people for their problems and was justifying it with the principle of personal responsibility. Sam was frightened. Even so, because of the trust he had established with Aren, his growth, and his own love for truth, he had the courage to step forward and speak for the first time in his life. He began to say that this didn't feel right to him, that it felt distorted. The more he tried to name what was wrong, the worse things got. He couldn't understand what was happening. He couldn't make sense of others' reactions or of his own. He couldn't do anything but follow the flow as it unfolded.

Finally, in an irrevocable moment, a woman stood up, glared at Sam, and said, "That's enough from you." Her words, her look, and her hands pushed Sam into his seat. The man who was leading the workshop came and placed his hands heavily on Sam's shoulders.

Sam looked around the room. He was wide-eyed as he surveyed all their faces. What he saw was hate. But he had no way of knowing it was the mask of fear. He could not fight them. He could not stand up to them. He went limp against the chair.

Upon his return home, dazed and spinning inside, Sam called for an emergency session with Aren. Once in his office, Sam felt safe enough to let down, to weep, to tremble. Aren held his feet to help him feel a connected presence and to keep him in his body while he journeyed with the feelings of the workshop experience. Sam wailed and wailed. "I'm the only one who saw it. Oh my God! No one else saw it. No one believed me 'cause no one else saw it."

The cycles of feeling came and went a few times, and then during a resting point Aren asked, "Sam, when did this happen before — that no one else saw something you saw? Don't think about it. Just let your feelings and the words 'Oh my God! No one else sees this' take you there."

Again and again Sam said the words, allowing the shock and the fear to take him back to a time when he was five years old. "What's happening, Sam?" asked Aren.

"There's a parade," said Sam. "The Emperor is walking down the street in the parade with nothing on but his underwear. I'm telling my mommy, 'The Emperor has nothing on at all!' My mommy is pulling me to her. She covers my mouth. My father puts his hands over hers. I look up and see that they hate me for what I've seen and for what I've said. I go dead inside."

Silence followed. It was as though Sam had been taken into a deep sleep lasting several long minutes. Then he stirred, wailing again, "What can you do, Aren, as a child or an adult, when you see something others don't see, don't want to see, don't want you to see?"

Aren was quiet. The silence lengthened as he sought a response that would do justice to the question. Finally he began, "Sam, there is so much unconsciousness in our world. This lack of self-awareness not just in others, but also in ourselves, is often a defense against feeling. Against truth. Even against love. Yes, even against that which we most want. Yet our inability to be fully conscious of our thoughts, feelings, and motivations causes great pain, to ourselves and also to others.

"People don't want to see, sense, feel, know — out of fear. Fear of ancient memories and feelings, which may come surging forth if they don't keep themselves deadened. Fear of the consequences in their present lives and in the future. But at the same time, Sam, our world, precisely because of its unconsciousness, desperately needs people with responsible conscious knowing. Our world needs for you to heal so that you can speak what you feel, what you sense, what you hear, and what you see. Our world needs for you to stay awake and aware and to show us where there is poison beneath the surface — or maybe even diamonds. Our world needs for you to cherish your sensitivity and your voice and to give us the truth from your heart.

"Don't let the world's attempts to keep you from revealing the truth frighten you. Heal whatever is in you, Sam, that blocks your way to revealing what you know. Remember, this is a gift we all need and that you deeply need to give."

"Oh my God! I can't believe it. You don't hate me for seeing and telling the truth. You treasure it as a sacred gift." Sam breathed deeply for a few moments, taking in this dream come true.

"Now can we talk about the specifics of what you saw at the workshop?" asked Aren. "What you saw that was so distorted? Tell me again what you sensed happening that didn't feel right."

So once again, this time with greater confidence and courage, Sam began to name what he had experienced. "The leader was twisting everything the participants brought to work on so as to blame them, and was justifying it with the principle of personal responsibility. He was telling people that if they had a problem, they had caused it and it was up to them to find out how to fix it. He didn't say it quite this directly, but he did say it."

"Good for you, Sam!" applauded Aren. "You knew you were experiencing the distortion of a sacred spiritual truth. This is a complex matter, but I will offer you all I can on the subject. And then you can find in you what resonates and where you need to go with it."

"I'm listening," answered Sam.

"The principle of personal responsibility is a profound truth, inviting us to look inside ourselves to find the basic causes of what is occurring in our lives. There are many spiritual seekers who believe we have no impact on our journeys, that fate is fate and we are at the mercy of our destiny. There are other spiritual students and teachers who believe that we have complete control of what happens in our lives, that destiny is solely a matter of cause and effect based on our feelings, thoughts, and actions both past and present.

"I think, Sam, that the truth is somewhere between these two perspectives. Those who believe we are at the mercy of our destiny are not aware of the profound effects the unconscious layers of our being have on our journeys. They don't know how to do the work to find within themselves the unconscious decisions that actually create what they call their destiny. And so, unaware that they could work to become more conscious of the forces that seem beyond their impact, they feel helpless, hopeless, and at the mercy of their destiny. Sometimes they even spiritualize this experience away by falsely naming it surrender. If only they were willing and able to become more conscious, they could free themselves.

"On the other hand, those who believe we have complete control over what happens in our lives, Sam, have distorted the principle of personal responsibility to maintain the illusion that they are in control. I have seen people who have experienced a positive impact of their inner work use this to reinforce their illusion of total control; I have witnessed as they have then turned around to blame and treat with disdain others who don't seem to be in control.

"The mistaken teaching is that we are responsible for *every* occurrence in our lives. The reason we want to believe that is to have control, so we will not feel again what we felt when we were children. This distortion creates a trap. It is a duplication of the wounded child's attempts to avoid the terror of lack of control by finding some ways, however illusory they might be, to try to be in control.

"Do you understand what I am saying, Sam?"

"Yes, Aren. It sounds like teachings that distort this tenet of personal responsibility may have drawn to them teachers and students who were abused as children. And since as children they desperately attempted to discover how to control an alcoholic mother or a father who beat or molested them, they are now desperately trying to use the principle itself to control those around them — and even life. This is how they believe they will create safety."

"You've got it! Now let's go on," continued Aren. "The distortions need to be untwisted. We need to allow for the many possibilities that exist here. I can name only *some* of the possibilities. Perhaps Spirit and Mystery will teach us others.

"Some things *are* our responsibility, Sam. And we need to heal those things to change our lives. Let's imagine that as a result of my ancient pain, I've decided I'm not good enough. Once I've made that decision, no matter how good I try to be, I will still believe and feel I'm not good enough. In addition, anytime I do something that is less than perfect, I will perceive it as *proving* I'm not good enough. In an instance like this, the healing comes from my taking the responsibility to change my decision. This means also going to the original experience during which I first made that decision and feeling the pain from which it came.

"Does this make sense, Sam?"

"Uh huh."

"Now some things *are* our responsibility, but we have misinterpreted their meaning and need to find new ways to understand. For example, a woman lives with a man who batters her. Every time he abuses her he tells her that if she were more loving, he wouldn't need to punish her. This dovetails with her own beliefs that she isn't loving and needs to be punished. And that's the responsibility she mistakenly takes in the situation.

"Perhaps many would agree with her, Sam, but that is the distorted meaning. The true responsibility she has here is to protect herself. She serves her own soul by refusing to allow her husband's abuse and also serves his soul in the process.

"Any questions here, Sam?"

"No, Aren. This is really helpful. Please keep going."

"Some things, Sam, are sent to us by Spirit simply to protect us, even though the form may seem unpleasant. Perhaps you are on your way up the coast to a winter vacation in the mountains and your nearly new car breaks down. You have taken good care of your car, yet you hear the bad news from the mechanic that it will take a week to repair. You are frustrated and discouraged, but you decide to stay in this coastal town for vacation instead of forging ahead. You wonder if there is anything in you that caused this 'mishap.' You search your soul. Are you afraid of pleasure? Are you punishing yourself for something unconsciously? Are you feeling guilty about something? You can't find a piece that is your responsibility, but you keep yourself open to knowing. Perhaps you hear on the news the next evening that there was an avalanche in the very mountain resort that had been your destination. And you are so grateful for the mystery of Spirit's protection. Or perhaps you never find out about the avalanche. In any case, because of your car's breakdown, you are safe. Who can explain that?"

"I never knew how many different facets of responsibility there are, Aren."

"Amazing, isn't it? Here's another one: Some things are part of the evolution of the group consciousness and beyond our individual ability to completely control.

"While every single bit of healing and transformation we do within ourselves affects the group consciousness and contributes to change in the world, we cannot make some changes alone. For example, I can use environmentally safe products in my life, affecting my neighborhood and wherever I go. But I cannot clean up the environment all over the world single-handedly. So also, Sam, I can find and heal the places in me that are uncaring and even cruel — we all have them. And I can help those who come to work with me do the same, which does affect the world. But I cannot alone remove uncaring and cruelty from our world, no matter how much I wish I could do so.

"Some years ago, Sam, I had an experience that helped me really understand this. My work had taken an unexpected turn, and I was going deeper and deeper with people. But very few people were wanting to go to the depths. Although I was joyously helping those who did come to do the work, I kept seeking to know if there was anything in me that was responsible for these small numbers. At times I felt afraid, frustrated, angry, and just mystified. In one of those phases, three colleagues in the period of a single week offered their support to me. None of them had spoken to the others. None of them knew each other. Yet each one said the same thing to me: 'It must be so difficult to be a pioneer, waiting to have people become ready for what you have to offer.' And each time I wept with relief to hear the truth. My only responsibility here was to stay true to myself and my vision, to hold the group consciousness until those who would be called were ready, and to help prepare the readiness wherever I was truly guided."

"What a powerful example, Aren!"

"Yes, Sam, it is. It was a powerful experience too. Now there's still one more piece I can offer here about personal responsibility. Some things are simply part of the mystery — the sacred mystery of life and of each soul's journey. Each of us is on a particular path in order to become conscious — to grow self-awareness, dissolve our defenses, heal our wounds, transform our distorted energies, and emerge as our true selves. This process and what happens in it are part of a soul's co-creation with the Divine.

"When things seem to be going amiss, we do need to look within, seek and find 'what is mine' calling to be healed and transformed; but we also need to develop the capacity to know 'what is not mine.' As with our dreams, this is a very personal discernment, unique for each of us. To impose some recipe or guide book upon that discernment would be a violation of the individual heart and soul."

Aren paused, indicating he was finished. He turned to look at the clock, "I see our time is about up for today, Sam. Maybe that's a good thing, for we've covered a lot of ground."

Sam stood. "This has been such a fruitful session, Aren. I have a lot to digest. Thank you for seeing me on such short notice." Sam shook Aren's hand and walked out the door.

HERE AND NOW

CHAPTER FIVE
YOU ARE RESPONSIBLE FOR EVERYTHING

Review . . .

The principle of personal responsibility is distorted beyond recognition into justification for blame.

Sam's parents silenced him as a child.

As a result, he grew up and was always afraid inside. At a workshop Sam attended, the well-known leader blamed the participants for their problems and justified the blame with "the principle of personal responsibility."

With the help of Aren, his spiritual therapist, Sam rode his feelings to earlier occurrences of this blame-responsibility scenario. Aren also gave Sam a motivating axiom for potential visionaries: "The world needs for you to heal, so that you can speak what you feel, what you sense, what you hear, and what you see."

Consider . . .

In the 1950's, while people were attaching stigma to therapy, that very same vehicle began to nourish in our world the bud of personal self-responsibility. As the bud grew, blights and bugs, perennially in the human garden, were attracted to and feasted on this tender new growth, disfiguring it. We still often ignore or fail to treat that which attacks the newly emerging capacity for authentic personal responsibility. This disfigurement has made it confusing and difficult for people to take responsibility for what is their own and hold others accountable for what is theirs.

❖ Think about your walk with self-responsibility. See if you can discover or name one aspect of yourself that serves to blight your own budding self-responsibility.

❖ Where are you clear and where are you muddled about your own responsibility for circumstances in your life?

❖ Does the confusion of others in your life about their accountability affect your ability to stay clear?

❖ Does blame, yours or another's, interfere with accurate assessment of responsibility?

❖ How does the damage to your self-responsibility impinge upon your thriving?

And Then . . .

Sam returned and continued his work with Aren. Longing, as Aren had said, to heal what blocked his way to revealing what he knew, Sam committed himself to bringing his gift of truth out into the world. His dedication and follow-through brought out the leader in Sam. Eventually, he became an elder in his family, a Senior Vice President at his corporation, and President of the Board of Trustees at his place of worship.

I'M POSITIVELY NOT GONNA DEAL WITH THE NEGATIVE

*F*inally, a block away from the castle, a little child's voice was heard saying, "But the Emperor has nothing on at all!" The child's father insisted, "Shhhhhhh!" The child's mother commanded, "Shhhhhhh!"

The child said, "But you told me always to tell the truth. That's what I'm doing!"

The child's father persisted, "Shhhhhhh!" The child's mother demanded with a louder "Shhhhhhhhhh!"

Then the child insisted, "But you told me always to tell the truth. Why aren't you telling the truth? Why now are you trying to stop me from telling the truth?"

The parents picked up the child, carried him out of the crowd, and took him home, refusing to say a word about what had happened. They fed him, played with him, bathed him, and read to him. They even sang him a lullaby.

At the end of the lullaby he asked his parents, "Why won't you talk to me about the naked Emperor?" His parents sang another lullaby. He tried one more time. "Mommy, Daddy, why do you teach me to tell the truth, but now that I am telling the truth, pretend I've said nothing?" His parents sang one more lullaby, kissed him on the cheek, tucked him in, and left the room.

In his bed all alone, the little child was in shock. He went to sleep in shock. He woke up in shock. At breakfast not a word was said about the *procession. In fact, never again did anyone say a word about the procession or the Emperor's nakedness. It was as though it had never existed.*

And the child began to forget what he knew. At first it seemed like a dream. Eventually, it didn't even exist in his consciousness. And the child forgot the truth.

Jason grew up. He did not remember the day the Emperor had nothing on at all. He saw and spoke the truth again and again because he could do no other. Not only had he been taught to tell the truth, it was his nature. But in response to his truth-telling, people ignored him or people pretended to ignore him. People wanted to address only the positive, rather than attend to all that is.

As the world entered the New Age, focusing solely on the positive became respected as though it were spiritual law. It was taught in psychological circles; it was taught in recovery circles; it was taught in spiritual circles: Be positive. Leave the negative alone. Dealing with the negative only feeds it and gives it energy.

This made no sense to Jason whatsoever. He didn't know what to do about it, though, and every attempt he made filled him with uneasiness.

Hoping to make peace with this dilemma, Jason began to see a psychotherapist, Malcolm, to work with his feelings. Malcolm appreciated Jason's willingness and desire to work with both the positive and the negative. He supported Jason's refusal to split them apart and further the world's duality — the tendency to create black and white opposites out of everything: dark and light, love and hate, good and evil.

For Jason, this was an unexpected treasure. After years of people's efforts to stop him from looking at "the negative," he never anticipated someone would support him in this way. He immersed himself in work with his own duality — positive and negative, yes and no, birth and death — and also with seeing and feeling the opposites in the world around him.

Some of what Jason was struggling with triggered uncomfortable stirrings in Malcolm despite his supportiveness. He began withdrawing from Jason at crucial points during their sessions, in both subtle and not-so-subtle ways. Jason could feel it. Jason could talk about it. And although he didn't know the technical term, it was Malcolm's transference of something from his past onto Jason.

But Malcolm was unaware of these lapses of presence and denied it when Jason called his attention to it. Each time Malcolm would "disappear" Jason would flag it until finally Malcolm opened himself to the possibility and agreed to talk about it with his own therapist and his supervisor.

Jason appreciated that Malcolm was finally seeing and saying "yes," but at the same time, he was hurt and angry that his therapist had not been working on these painful happenings at his own initiation. After all, Malcolm was the therapist!

Malcolm didn't want to hear this. He accused Jason of being "too negative." Jason's truth-telling was being rejected again. And by his therapist, the man who had been supporting him all along to work with both the positive and the negative.

Although hurting, Jason thought he might have a better chance of reaching Malcolm if he began on a light note. "Malcolm, remember that old song?" And while he didn't have a very good singing voice, Jason sang, "You gotta accentuate the positive and eliminate the negative, latch onto the affirmative, and don't mess with Mr. In-Between."

Malcolm sat stone-faced.

Jason, who had grown in all ways, including courage, insisted to Malcolm that they leave no stone unturned in resolving this discord between them. Jason did not want to leave anything unresolved beneath the surface to undermine their relationship. But Malcolm could not join Jason in this endeavor: He could support Jason in holding together the positive and negative when it related to someone else; but Malcolm was unable to do the same when it was between Jason and himself. He wanted to know only the good about himself.

Once again, Jason saw and spoke the truth. In denial, Malcolm distanced himself from Jason. Rather than sacrifice his integrity, Jason knew he had to stop his work with Malcolm. Jason attempted to create a good-bye process that would honor what went well between them as well as acknowledge the cause for his leaving.

Malcolm turned the tables on Jason, unable to be involved in the goodbye at all. "You've changed, Jason. You're not the truth-seeker you were when you began with me."

On one level, Jason felt stronger and more sure of himself than ever. On another level, he was distraught. In his grief, he left his final session with Malcolm and drove to the ocean to find answers. Sitting on the beach, letting the sight and the sound of the waves move through his being, Jason descended into sobs.

After a few minutes of this, he felt a soft hand on his shoulder. Turning around, he thought he was seeing an angel. It was Mita. She asked, "May I be of help?"

He responded, still weeping, "I don't know."

But she kept her hand on his shoulder, and he let her. And she breathed to the rhythm of the waves, just as he wept to the same beat. When the dance was over, he thanked her softly, gently. And she thanked him back for allowing her to help.

She asked what was troubling him. And he explained what he could. He told her of his passion to know the truth and live the truth and the pain and difficulty of doing that when others around him don't.

"Dear Jason," she responded, "I know this dilemma well. Here's a story that I think will show you my knowing and help you feel the kin-dredness of real truth-tellers.

"One day, long ago, I saw a beautiful professional video. I was so touched by the sensitivity of the producer, Alan Burrows, a psychoana-lyst, that I reached out through a phone call to thank him.

"I spoke with him of my concern about the destructiveness taught and practiced in the name of growth, healing, and consciousness. I spoke of my own calling to address and help stop that harm, invited Alan's support, and offered mine to him.

"Alan's response was deeply disturbing to me. He explained he did not want to focus his energy on the damaging teachings in the New Age world. His reason was that in his experience if you try to stop a negative activity, you further empower that very activity.

"Jason, even though I could feel a huge 'no' pulsing through me, I didn't know what to say. But through the next week that 'no' remained so strong that I finally decided to write to him. With care, respect, and honesty, I told him all that I had appreciated about him and his response to me. But I also expressed to him my troubling, unrelenting feeling about his explanation.

"Describing to him my previous experience with this philosophy, including that in New Age circles, I added my distress at hearing it from him. With passion, I voiced the destructiveness of the philosophy itself. I pointed out that he was choosing to turn away from what I would call the lower self — what he calls the shadow — rather than transform it within and without.

"Isn't this exactly the kind of choice that allowed Hitler to come to power? Hitler's Germany would have been impossible without person after person choosing to not stop what was happening. I urged Burrows to resist colluding with evil, inside or outside, under the guise of not feeding it!"

"What did he write back?" asked Jason with eagerness.

"Most important, Jason," Mita answered enthusiastically, "is the effect of the experience on me. It added to the fire of my commitment to hold both the positive and the negative together, refusing to separate them or split them apart. I hold together peace and violence, joy and sorrow, doing and being. Alan Burrows separates them and other pairs of the positive and negative. His intention is to focus only on the positive. He mistakenly believes that as a result he will avoid the negative. Instead, splitting the two sides of the whole causes exactly what he was trying to avert — further empowering the negative."

"I'm glad the experience inspired you, Mita, but did he write back?" Jason returned to the essence of his question.

"Alan wrote back a brief note saying that he received and respected my truth and hoped I would respect his. His phrase, 'This is my truth and that is your truth,' actually muddies the meaning of 'truth,' Jason. Maybe Alan would say it is his truth, but the greater truth is that turning away from the negative actually colludes with it under a guise of not empowering it. And I can't muddy *this* truth.

"Statements such as 'This is my truth and that is your truth, and we can agree to disagree,' offer an escape from the need to do the hard work to know, learn, and face an objective truth, a deeper truth.

"For example, Jason," Mita continued, "do you know the story about the Emperor's new clothes?"

"No," replied Jason, "tell me."

And Mita began to tell Jason the story. He listened, spellbound. Eventually Mita came to the part …

"Finally, a block away from the castle, a little child's voice was heard saying, 'But the Emperor has nothing on at all!' "

Jason's whole body jerked. Tears flowed. Sounds poured forth through his throat from deep hollow caverns within. And Mita stayed with him. And Mita stayed with him. And Mita stayed with him.

More alive, more awake, more present than he had been for years, Jason turned to Mita and said, "That little boy was me!" His tears and his laughter played with one another for a long, long time. And then, "That is why this scenario has been such a painful one for me!"

"Yes, Jason. Congratulations! You have found the origin of your discomfort."

Mita paused for a long, silent moment. Then, "You know, Jason, during this time with you, I have discovered a discomfort for myself. I've supported your desire to not split the world into opposites. This is very difficult to teach and I have failed to live what I taught you.

"I can feel and hear that I have made myself good and Alan Burrows bad in this process. Personally, I need to explore that further for myself. I don't want to separate the inner and the outer. When we take on an action like my teaching you about splits, that is an outer expression of knowledge that lives within me. In addition to teaching you, it is also my responsibility to live what I teach, which is the inner component. Many teachers only 'talk the talk,' as the saying goes. It is a teacher's responsibility to go beyond that and 'walk the walk.' I will follow through, Jason, on the paradox that while teaching you about not splitting the good from the bad, I created a split in my own mind and heart. My work now is to heal that specific split so that I can practice what I preach."

Mita gazed into the distance and her voice grew reflective. "On a larger scale, this experience raises a profound question for us all: How do we point out and set right something that is amiss in the world without splitting the positive and the negative apart?"

HERE AND NOW

CHAPTER SIX
I'M POSITIVELY NOT GONNA DEAL WITH THE NEGATIVE

Review . . .

New Age seekers and practitioners, among others, create harm rather than growth and healing by addressing only the positive.

Jason, whose parents "shhhhhhhh-ed" him into denying the truth as a child, came up against the New Age spiritual principle prevalent in psychological, recovery, and spiritual circles: "Dealing with the negative only feeds it and gives it energy."

A wise woman, Mita, appeared like an angel to Jason and taught him how the same dynamic has occurred over and over in history, allowing world tragedies like Nazi Germany to occur. She helped Jason see that rather than turn away from "the shadow side," as New Age philosophies teach, he needed to heal the inner split between the positive and the negative.

Consider . . .

In Chapter Six, we came face-to-face with our tendency as humans to split ourselves, others, the world, and life apart into polar opposites — male/female, black/white, love/hate, peace/ violence, good/bad. This kind of polarization causes us to disown parts of the spectrum that lives within us.

Splitting into polar opposites inherently leads to misuse and abuse of power. Once we have rejected the part of us that hates, for example, we can see only love within us and hate in the world outside us. The part of us that hates secretly continues to drive us from the depths of our being, where we have buried the hate. As a result, refusing to acknowledge that we act out of hate, we scapegoat others. It is very likely that under the guise of love a person may do terrible things to others who seem hateful, as a way to banish the disowned hate.

❖ Reflect on history and think about the leaders who instigated burning at the stake those they named as witches — people who held sacred the earth, the feminine, the inherent worth and dignity of every person. The "burners" had outlawed in themselves and others like them those very connections that the "witches" experienced on a daily basis.

Think about the leader of a country who describes his nation as peace-loving while bombing the country next door.

Consider a corporation that donates millions to the environment but destroys the rain forest in order to benefit its bottom line.

Imagine a parent who beats his child while insisting, "This is for your own good."

❖ To redress the instances of power abuse that are the result of polarization, we need to go to the root and heal the split. Over time, become aware of the ways you polarize, explore your life as far back as you can remember, and name the ways in which you have created splits. For now, see if the examples in the chapter help you invite into

consciousness one place in your life where you have suffered from a split of your own making or of someone
else's making.

And Then . . .

Jason felt called to become an interfaith minister. This way he could
have a means for teaching many people about the healing of splits.
During his studies, Jason worked with a spiritual advisor who was able
to know, feel, and hold the different sides of a split, whether within himself, his students, or the world at large. This relationship helped Jason
thrive in his teaching and ministering.

THE SILENT TREATMENT

*F*inally, *a block away from the castle, a little child's voice was heard saying, "But the Emperor has nothing on at all!"*

The Emperor flew toward her, shouting, "Who do you think you are!

"How dare you question my authority!

"How dare you accuse me of wrongdoing!

"There must be something terribly wrong with you!

"How dare you question my truth!

"Off to prison with you! Off to the crazy house! Off with your head!

"I will make a lesson out of you, my dear!"

And the little girl was burned at the stake for saying what was really happening.

No one came forth to defend her.

No one came forth to protect her.

No one came forth to rescue her.

The whole town, her parents included, feared for their own lives and let her die . . . simply for telling what was really happening.

Lilly grew up. She no longer remembered the day the Emperor had nothing on at all. It was in another life. And now she was in this one.

Her father in this life had been a "rage-aholic." He had been the favorite in a family in which the firstborn male was treated like a god. He had expected everyone he came into contact with to treat him like God. Any threat to his idealistic illusion of himself was ill-advised. Any challenge to his authority, his power, his name, his will brought forth volcanic rage. He saw his wife, his children, his friends, his co-workers as mere servants. He ruled rather than related, and he ruled as a tyrant. Even a child's innocent question or comment evoked his spewing venom.

Throughout her childhood and early adulthood, Lilly had been terrified in his presence, so much so that she dared not allow herself to feel her terror. She had led the life of a numbed servant, aware of nothing deeper and of no other possibility.

Lilly couldn't wait to start her first real job as a secretary so she could afford her own apartment in a nearby city, just to get away from her oppressive father. Now, in her early 30's, with a matured perspective, she was seeing her father as never before. As she admitted to herself her father's cruelty, she began to change. As she named her father's abuse of power, a doorway opened to the feelings she had locked away for so many years. The depth and intensity of feeling were more than she could face on her own.

One day, as she was trying to hold all of her thoughts, feelings, and awareness, a friend at work stopped by her desk to share an article in a magazine. On the page opposite the article was an advertisement for a spiritual center by the ocean. It caught Lilly's attention, and she felt so strongly drawn to it that she went to visit the center over the weekend. After the first day there, she was sure this was a place where she could work through the feelings and her relationship with her father in a way that would keep her connected with Spirit.

The people at the center were warm and welcoming, staff and seekers alike. Lilly had weekly appointments with her spiritual advisor, Athena, a leader in the center's community. She was grateful to have found Athena, who was bringing into a more masculine-oriented center the energy and possibility of the Goddess. Because Lilly had decided to honor the Goddess in her own life, the connection with Athena seemed more and more a good match.

In her sessions with Athena, Lilly explored her relationship with the Goddess and the wounds in her history blocking that connection. They talked, prayed, created and performed rituals. Lilly did deep emotional release work, drew, danced, and wrote in her journal. After some months, Lilly felt safer to feel; but she also knew she had only scratched the surface.

Athena urged her to join a healing group for men and women, and soon Lilly felt safe enough to say "yes." Things went well for a while, but before long the people in the group grew unsupportive of her. When she came forth to work, she could feel them turn off. Maggie would play with her cuticles. Evan would tap his hand on the arm of his chair. Priscilla would just sit silently, her head cocked to the right, watching Lilly. Ann would roll her eyes. Susan and Sandra would whisper with each other. Alexander would recline on the pillows and often doze. They didn't do this when anyone else in the group began to speak. Eventually, Lilly started feeling a pain in her heart and womb. Week after week, she wished Athena would intervene. She wished that at least someone would comment on Athena's silence. It was as though the spiritual community had come to treat Athena like a goddess, not just a woman named for a goddess!

After a couple months, Lilly asked the group what was happening. All but one of the other participants justified their disrespectful behavior by blaming Lilly for something. Evan accused Lilly of having a fake smile. Maggie was angry whenever Lilly had Athena's attention. Ann thought Lilly's work in the group was nonsense. Susan didn't believe Lilly's feelings were genuine. Sandra didn't want to hear any more from Lilly. Alexander wished Lilly would leave the group.

Through all this Athena said not a word. Lilly had stopped wishing for Athena's help. Although it was painful, it felt normal, congruent with what she knew of life. She had spent her whole life responsible for protecting herself.

Finally, Lilly turned to the last woman, Priscilla.

"I am frightened of you, Lilly," Priscilla began, this time with her head cocked to the left. "You feel so deeply and intensely. You express your feelings so fully. Whenever I'm with you, my own feelings are evoked. That terrifies me. I can't be in your presence without feeling things I don't want to feel." And Priscilla bowed her head.

Could it be? Priscilla was taking responsibility for her own uncomfortable feelings, when Lilly's honest work evoked them, instead of blaming Lilly.

Lilly wept with relief. She looked at the others one by one. Each one's eyes were hard and cold. She turned back to Priscilla, who had lifted her head, and saw openness on her face.

"Thank you so much, Priscilla," Lilly whispered through her tears. "Thank you for not blaming me for feelings that are your own. I grew up being attacked for even an innocent question. To me your honesty and self-responsibility are priceless."

Priscilla smiled and nodded, her own eyes bright with tears of compassion.

Lilly continued, "Priscilla, you have helped me understand that I have done nothing to deserve the disrespect of the group. My doing exactly what Athena has taught me simply evoked something in all the rest of you. I thank the Goddess for your integrity and your help to know this truth."

Once again, Athena said nothing.

In the following two sessions, the group members continued their disrespectful behavior and Athena remained silent. Lilly wondered if she should leave the group and the center. Was she staying because there was something important that was to happen here? Or was it because this was so much her ancient experience that leaving was not really an option she was capable of enacting?

In their next private session, Lilly said she wanted to talk with Athena about the damaging effects of her silence. Athena called this transference and insisted that Lilly regress to childhood and have a pretend conversation with her father about things he was doing that didn't feel good to her.

This technique was part of what Lilly had learned at the center, and she knew it was a valuable tool in healing. But it felt like Athena was using the technique as a way to avoid the discussion between them. Although Lilly didn't want to do that, she was, unfortunately, still in the grip of the abuse dynamic, and she obediently did as Athena demanded.

After doing that part of the work, Lilly still wanted to speak with Athena about her silence. Athena did not want to hear anything about herself.

Something that had been growing and healing in Lilly over so much time finally clicked into place. She was clear that Athena had been using a regal silence to abdicate her responsibility as a spiritual leader. Lilly knew this was a subtle form of abuse of power that was normalized, accepted, and fed by a community that idolized Athena.

Lilly also began to see and wonder about the subtleties in the situation: Athena had really been condoning the group's mistreatment of Lilly. Was Athena getting a thrill out of seeing someone actively abused while appearing innocent herself?

"If you refuse to talk about this, Athena, then I cannot work with you anymore!"

Athena said nothing, and Lilly left.

Without ties to the center, she found herself adrift, wanting help, but not trusting in spiritual leadership at all! For months she worked on her own to heal this new layer of wounding. Athena and Lilly's father looked like they behaved in very different ways, yet underneath they were both tyrants. How could she ever end the re-enactment of this abuse?

Lilly's own Spirit began to visit her in her dreams. While her human name was Lilly, she called her Spirit Mita. Mita helped Lilly to see and know when abuse was occurring. She promised to help Lilly heal within herself anything that could invite abusiveness. And she assisted Lilly in developing her strength, courage, and ability to confront abusiveness when she saw it.

For the sake of Lilly's knowledge, and in case she might enter therapy or spiritual work again, Mita taught her that in healing and spiritual therapies it is important to uncover and work through the client's transference of the past onto the present. But it is equally vital to the integrity of the process to identify and resolve difficulties that are occurring in the current time, sometimes due to the transference of the therapist onto the client, called "counter-transference." Mita explained that to concentrate on only one side of this equation plays out as a misuse of power and often creates abuse of the client. The therapist needs to explore, if only with his own supervisor and therapist, both his own transference and counter-transference. She added that it is not as easy to identify counter-transference when someone is silent, but it may still be there.

Lilly was grateful for all that Mita was offering and teaching within these extraordinary dreams. Yet, Lilly was still terrified, right down to her cells. And she didn't know why. She had identified Athena's abusive silence, and she had confronted this abuse when she saw it. She had done so much work with her child-self related to her father's abusiveness. Why was terror still living within her?

She asked these questions each night before sleeping, opening herself to Mita's help. One night, Lilly had a dream in which she heard Mita's voice saying, "Remember this?" And then something akin to a movie began. Lilly saw two seemingly fine men talking with an Emperor, seducing him into buying new garments, which they would weave. The garments had a special quality, according to the men, such that anyone who was flawed in character or unfit for office would not be able to see the clothes.

Lilly watched as the fake tailors pulled the wool over the eyes of the entire court, Emperor included, and the entire town, with the exception of one little girl.

And as the little girl spoke, Lilly was no longer watching the movie, but became part of it. "But the Emperor has nothing on at all!" little Lilly exclaimed.

The Emperor flew toward her shouting, "Who do you think you are!

"How dare you question what I'm doing!

"Something is terribly wrong with you, my dear, not me!

"Off to prison with you!"

And Lilly, age five, was burned at the stake for saying what was really happening. Not one soul came forth to defend her. The whole town, her parents included, feared for their own lives and let her die — simply for telling what was really happening.

Lilly awakened herself screaming and shaking the terror out of her depths. She screamed and screamed. She trembled for hours. She felt Mita's presence. And she knew! Now she knew why the experience of abuse in any form, why the speaking and naming of what was happening was so very frightening to her.

Now, hopefully, she could put that part of her lifetimes to rest.

HERE AND NOW

CHAPTER SEVEN
THE SILENT TREATMENT

Review . . .

Spiritual and other counselors often distort the psychological principle of transference, creating an imbalance between therapist and client and refusing to confront their own counter-transference.

Lilly's father was a rage-aholic, ruling his family as a tyrant rather than relating as a parent. As a young adult, Lilly went to a spiritual center for help. But in group sessions, a community leader, Athena, met Lilly's work on herself with a damaging silence. When Lilly wanted to talk about it, Athena called her feelings transference. Lilly was caught in the abuse dynamic. Her healer was the abuser.

Mita, Lilly's own Spirit, came to her in dreams and facilitated her healing. She helped Lilly know when abuse was occurring and helped her develop the strength and courage to confront the abuse.

Consider . . .

Sometimes abuse of power is out in the open and blatant. Other times it is under the cover of inaction and silent refusal to protect those in our care.

Both types of abuse in childhood commonly result in a lack of clarity, a kind of paralysis, and a lack of self-trust in the face of current-day abuse of power.

Children are surrounded by people who are more powerful and who are supposed to be more powerful than they are. Most of us, during childhood, have had some experiences with adults in our lives misusing or abusing their power in relation to us.

❖ Discover for yourself where you were wounded by abuse of power in your childhood.

❖ Name a place where the abuse was obvious and another where it was insidious.

❖ Allow yourself to remember the experiences of numbness or paralysis you have had in your adult life as a result of those early imprints.

And Then . . .

Lilly moved into the next phase of her life, relieved by solving the mystery of her response to abuse of power. Although she felt skittish about entering into therapy or spiritual work after her experience with Athena, Lilly knew that at the right time, and with the right therapist, she might well take that step. For now, she was content to continue her dream-time relationship with Mita and to practice in her everyday world what she had already learned.

ABRACADABRA ALACAZAM! – ALL GRIEF BE GONE

Finally, a block away from the castle, a little child's voice was heard saying, "But the Emperor has nothing on at all!"

The Emperor heard the child's statement ring throughout the town. He turned around, walked purposefully toward the little girl. Arriving in front of her, he squatted before her. He met her eyes with his own and then looked down to find a baby in her arms. He reached for the baby, and the little girl held tight to her beloved brother. He tugged at the baby, and the little girl screamed, "No!"

Snatching the baby out of her arms, the Emperor trumpeted to the townspeople, "This baby will be the fitting sacrifice for a little girl's impudence." Turning again to the girl, he threatened, "The next time you are tempted to be so full of yourself, child, you will be brought to your knees by the memory of this sacrifice."

And the Emperor drowned the baby in the fountain, right there in the center of town. The girl screamed and wept until she could no longer, and then she fell into a deep sleep.

Emmy grew up. She no longer remembered the day the Emperor had nothing on at all.

She met and married a loving, honest man named Alex. They were soul mates, loving and supporting each other, helping each other grow, praying and playing together, and celebrating the divine essence of everything in the world.

Eventually, in just the right timing, and out of their deep love, Emmy became pregnant. In due time, they had a beautiful little girl. They were thrilled with the entire process. The nine months together, preparing themselves and the little baby within Emmy's womb, was a rich, nourishing period of their lives.

Everything proceeded beautifully. The birth in their own home was magnificent with all parties fully alive and present. Bless the midwife they had found. She helped make the process more natural, more loving, even more sacred than they had envisioned.

Alex and Emmy grew with joy into their new tasks and routines of life with baby Pauline. They loved co-parenting as an aspect of their partnership. It taught them so much about themselves and each other. And they delighted in the everyday moments that were part of seeing Pauline, attuning to her, loving her, and helping her become all that she could be. Not that there weren't any challenges in the process. They just felt so grateful to have each other and their daughter.

Their longing to have another baby began soon after Pauline's birth. Alex and Emmy had to help each other be patient, as they waited till the right time. When Pauline was 18 months old, Emmy discovered she was pregnant. Both parents were elated.

This pregnancy had a different quality to it. After all, Pauline was a vibrant, active toddler. It was, nonetheless, a delicious time in their lives, and when Stuart was born, Emmy and Alex felt contentment beyond words.

One night, several weeks after his birth, awakened by the baby's cry, Emmy went into the nursery to find Stuart shrieking. Then suddenly he fell silent. Frozen by the side of the crib, holding a limp and lifeless baby Stuart in her arms, again and again she screamed, "No!" Alex and little Pauline were awakened into a world of horror by Emmy's screaming. And nothing was ever the same again.

Stuart, who had died so suddenly and inexplicably, became to Emmy her only child. Hour after hour, day after day, she sat by his crib weeping and talking to him as though he were still there. And Pauline, the toddler who lived, became to Alex his only child. Grief-stricken himself, he took care of Pauline day and night. He cried for the loss of Stuart but turned his heart to Pauline. Emmy and Alex were living two different lives. It seemed as though Emmy had died with Stuart. And Alex's greatest loss was his soul mate.

He talked to her. He cried with her. He prayed for her. He begged her. It was not that she didn't hear him. It was not that she didn't want to respond to him. Something huge had taken over her life, her heart, her soul — something she could not explain, something over which she had no control.

Finally, in desperation, Alex arranged for them to be on a television show to get some help from a panel of healers. Each day's show of *Healers in Action* consisted of people in the audience getting help from one or more of three practicing healers. There was a new panel each week. Sometimes the healers were of international acclaim, and other times they were locals. Alex had seen the show and was excited by it. Going on the show gave them both a shred of hope.

After their story was told for all the world to know, the healers took turns, one by one, offering their advice to Emmy and Alex. The first one told Emmy, "You can only indulge your grief for so long, Dear One, and then you have to move on. You just have to pull yourself up by your bootstraps and do whatever you have to do. If you don't, you are cheating yourself and your family out of your presence."

Emmy wanted to scream! Instead she practically whispered to compensate for the urge to scream: "Don't you understand? I have no control over this. It is bigger than I am, and I don't know what 'it' is."

The panelist answered her question, his best compassionate mask covering his contempt for Emmy's lack of control. "My dear, it is not that you have no control over this, but rather that you refuse to take control of yourself here. You are enjoying wallowing in the mud of your grief."

Emmy bowed her head and choked back her rage and shame in the face of the healer's humiliating her on worldwide television. She didn't know what to do. She had a sense of this man and knew that if she said something, if she got up and left, he would humiliate her more. She wished she had never let Alex persuade her to come on this show.

The second healer came in at this point in an attempt to move away from what was happening and to repair some of the damage. With her good-hearted intention, she didn't realize she too was about to cause Emmy harm.

The healer spoke to Alex and Emmy, explaining to them that Stuart was not just a baby, but also a spirit. She tried to get them to focus their attention on the spirit that came into this life as a baby boy named Stuart. She explained that even though Stuart's death was shocking and painful, great gifts could come of their experience with him, both while he was alive and also through his death. "Turn away from the grief and look for the gifts with gratitude," she advised. "Otherwise you will be refusing the blessings offered to you."

Emmy squirmed inside her skin. It seemed as though the healer were saying there was no reason for Emmy to feel grief, and she knew there was a reason. That Stuart was a spirit would not magically take her grief away. She was already feeling guilty enough for her inability to move through it. What the panelist was saying only increased her guilt. Once again, not wanting to bring more onto herself, she remained quiet.

'This is making matters worse,' Emmy thought, as the third healer went on in the same vein as the second. 'He is talking only about Stuart's gifts as a soul. What about his gifts as a human infant? His sweetness, his innocence, his purity that opened my heart even wider than ever before? Am I not supposed to grieve the loss of that? If only these spiritual healers could take seriously this half of what Stuart's life and death mean,' she anguished silently.

Until now, the master of ceremonies had been a silent presence. At this point, with just a few minutes left before the end of the show, he turned to the healers and thanked them for their spiritual wisdom and power. Then he looked at Alex and Emmy and said to them, "Don't you feel absolutely blessed by the power today's panelists have brought to you?"

With tears in his eyes, Alex, who had missed the damage that had been done, was satisfied to walk away with the one seed of truth that gave him hope — that Stuart was a spirit, too. Feeling sickened by the emcee's calling this real power, Emmy had the presence to realize that she, her feelings, her essence, and the essence of Stuart were what was really being ignored. Emmy knew it would be fruitless to speak and so remained silent. She knew if she spoke the truth, it would once again be spiritual-ized away.

Weeping at Stuart's grave that evening, Emmy found herself in the presence of an angel? a god? No, simply a wise, loving man, who was at the cemetery for his own reasons. His name, Emmy discovered, was Aren. He knelt to the left and a little behind Emmy, and when she turned to see him, asked kindly, "Can I help in any way?"

"I wish you could. I lost my son two years ago," replied Emmy, ges-turing toward the headstone. "And I have been in unrelenting mourning ever since. It is like a maze with no way out. It's caused me to lose not only my son, Stuart, but also my daughter, Pauline, and my husband, Alex. At the end of our rope, we went on a popular television show today, where the guest healers basically missed my essence, missed my grief, and 'guilted' me into rising above my feelings. Their teaching that the way to honor my child is to think of him as a soul implies it is wrong to mourn the loss of my very real baby. By my silence I pretended I understood and would follow their guidance. But Aren, I cannot. When you say 'can't' to those spiritual gurus, they just tell you, 'It's not that you can't but that you won't. If you're doing it, there must be some gain in it for you.' My God! Aren, I don't know where to turn."

"Dear Emmy," Aren replied. "For now, you may turn to me. I have walked many miles with mourning, my own and that of others near me. Mourning has its own organic timing and rhythm. That needs to be honored. There may be spiritual meaning in a loss experience, and we may need to grow through the experience. But we cannot spiritualize the loss and the grief away. Doing so only represses the experience, blocks the flow of the life force through us, and creates the imperative to deal with the grief later.

"I am familiar with the work of numerous spiritual healers on the program. Many of their teachings are profound. Others are quite distorted. The problem is the healers on the show you attended didn't meet you in your grief, to be with you and to be sure you were in the process of going through it. Instead, even the kinder ones encouraged you to rise above it. I grieve, Emmy, when I see spiritual teachers misuse their power to invite people to rise above the human, whether they do it consciously or unconsciously, with intention or out of ignorance. And I weep that this encouragement for premature transcendence magnetizes so many people, precisely because they are so afraid to feel their feelings! Sadly, Emmy, in our world, mourning itself is not honored or given its rightful place in life. Without mourning, the human and spiritual process of death and rebirth cannot rightly occur.

"Your soul, it seems to me, is calling out for help and support to mourn fully. Others may want us to cry for a time and then get on with it, back to function-mode, while we feel like walking the streets aimlessly, wrapped in black cloth, ripping and wailing till we can no more, knowing we are protected by the watchful, heartful eyes of the community."

"Could such a community exist?" asked Emmy with more life in her voice and face than had been there for ages.

"For now, Emmy, only where we create it with those who understand with their hearts as well as their heads. But with our help, perhaps someday it will exist in our world again as it once did long ago. Would you like me to help you create it?"

"Oh yes! Aren. That would mean so much to me."

So Aren gathered a compassionate community on behalf of Emmy and her need for mourning. Alex was invited, but he could not bear to participate. Emmy stayed with Aren and the others for weeks, living and expressing the depths of her agonizing grief. The change in her was breathtaking. Yet the path out of the maze was still hidden.

One day she and Aren were sitting by the lake and Aren said, "Emmy, this time you have spent actively, openly mourning has worked wonders for you; yet it seems that at this point you are somehow stuck in the grief. My instinct tells me that you can't find your way out because there is an ancient grief buried within you of which you are not conscious. Grief ungrieved comes back to haunt us. And future griefs inevitably evoke the old unresolved ones. If my hunch is accurate and it is right for you, we may be able to identify an ancient grief. Would you be interested in doing an exploration with me to see if we can discover where you are stuck and free you?"

"Please, Aren. Help me out of this maze."

"All right, Emmy. Let's see what we can do. Close your eyes and begin feeling your grief. Now express it aloud."

Emmy began to moan softly. "As you do," Aren continued, "let that very expression take you down, down, down through a spiral of feeling and energy into another time in your soul's journey. Another time when you were also filled with grief. Just follow the spiral, Emmy, and let's see where it takes you."

"I'm six years old. I'm wailing and screaming. The Emperor is drowning my baby brother, because I dared to speak the truth. Because I dared to say, 'The Emperor has nothing on at all.' I weep for days, for weeks, for months. I beg my mother to drown me so that I don't have to live with the pain anymore. But my mother refuses, saying she loves me with all her heart and wants me to live. And, besides, it wasn't my fault — it was the Emperor who did something distorted and cruel."

Emmy and Aren talked for a while, marveling that here was the clue. Here was the meaning. Here was the root of her seemingly endless mourning. Now she would be able to honor both Stuart the baby and Stuart the spirit. Suddenly Emmy began to laugh with relief and delight. Laughter — for the first time in years! What a beautiful sound.

Although she could barely wait to go home and tell Alex, Emmy stayed long enough to express appreciation to Aren for her newfound ability to live with joy and grief, and for his help, which was a gift of grace.

HERE AND NOW

CHAPTER EIGHT
ABRACADABRA ALACAZAM!
– ALL GRIEF BE GONE

Review . . .

So-called spiritual healers can distort the process of grief, urging people to rise above their emotions and short-circuit the grieving process. Lives can be irretrievably turned inside out when the bereavement process is incomplete, whatever the loss.

When Emmy was a child, the Emperor of the land snatched her brother from her because she dared to tell the truth about the ruler.

Grief drove Emmy and her soul mate, Alex, apart after the death of their second child. By discounting Emmy's grief and agonizing pain, a panel of healers on a television show reinforced the unhealthy cultural pattern of stunting one's grief process.

A wise, loving man named Aren appeared at the grave of Emmy's son and showed her that mourning has organic timing and rhythm. Aren helped Emmy follow her feelings to their roots for the sake of healing and transformation. His teaching: "Without mourning, the human and spiritual process of death and rebirth cannot occur."

Consider . . .

To grieve thoroughly is not truly honored or supported in many cultures. People are afraid of grief's power, its intensity, and its depth. People are afraid of the passage into the unknown that grieving requires.

Many have come to me while sorrowing for their losses. Their anguish is compounded by the lack of support and the isolation they feel.

I offer them a box of black cloths, inviting them to rip the cloths to shreds. They are amazed and relieved at my openhearted invitation. I assure them that my office is a safe space in which to wail and wail. I support them in taking their own time and following their own pace through the mourning process. I tell them, "If at any point we find you are stuck in the grief, I will work with you to discover how and where you are stuck and help you move once again." As a result, they are freed to follow their grief through the darkness back into the light.

Secure in the knowledge that even extreme grief can be safely expressed in such a sacred space, they are ready to accept that mourning is needed not only when we lose someone through death, but also for many kinds of losses — the end of a marriage, the loss of a job, the failure of a project, even the growing up of the children we have so loved and helped to fly.

As Emmy showed us, our lives can become irretrievably turned inside out if we do not complete the bereavement process when faced with a loss. The consequences of the interruption of the process are serious and may even cause harm. Anyone in a position of power with a grieving person needs to be exquisitely careful to support the organic process of the grieving. The spiritualizing or premature transcendence imposed upon Emmy is a common way people interfere with the grieving process.

❖ Have you ever witnessed an interruption in the mourning of another person?

❖ Have you had any losses you feel you have been unable to grieve fully?

❖ Can you name factors that for you might have been obstacles to thorough grieving?

❖ Are you aware of the effects in your life of the uncompleted mourning?

❖ How have you interfered with grieving, whether your own or someone else's?

These are complex questions. Trust that if you cannot answer every question to your own satisfaction, the answers are nevertheless incubating in the safe and private places deep within yourself.

And Then . . .

Emmy returned home, having mourned not only the loss of her son, Stuart, but also that of her baby brother. She was present again. She was available again. She was able to connect with her daughter, Pauline, and her husband, Alex, again . . . at last. But now she could see that Alex wasn't truly accessible and so encouraged him to enter into his grieving.

JUST MOVE ON

*F*inally, a block away from the castle, a little child's voice was heard saying, "But the Emperor has nothing on at all!" Another child, a few feet away, heard the voice of truth and gazed upon her in awe. He was about to reach out to her when he saw the Emperor approaching.*

The Emperor squatted in front of the girl and looked her straight in the eye. The little boy watched as the Emperor took the girl's baby brother out of her arms and drowned him in the town fountain, claiming him as the sacrifice for her impudence. The little boy went home that night with the memory of the baby's death and the little girl's cries and screams ringing in his ears and in his heart.

For days he did everything he could to silence those sounds. He helped his father. He helped his mother. Most successfully, he took care of his own baby brother, whose living, growing laughter seemed gradually to replace the haunting cries of the little girl.

Alex grew up. He no longer remembered the day the Emperor had nothing on at all.

He married his first love. They had a wonderful relationship until one day several weeks after their second child was born, his wife, Emmy, found the baby, Stuart, shrieking and then dead in his crib.

The loss of his son was enormous. But what was truly earth-shattering was the loss of his wife. Emmy fell into grief so profound that Alex could not help her. And as he heard her weep and wail and scream, he had an irresistible compulsion to turn all his love toward his still-living daughter, Pauline.

Finally, after what seemed an eternity of grief and disconnection, Emmy found assistance from a compassionate man named Aren. He helped Emmy go all the way through the mourning process until, finally, one day Emmy came to Alex with a smile on her face. Aren had helped her find where she was stuck in her mourning. It was a mystery no more.

Emmy told Alex of the day the Emperor had nothing on at all. She told him of her seeing it, knowing it, and saying it. She told him of the Emperor's response, his making a sacrifice of her baby brother, and of her excruciating grief. And with each word she said, Alex's missing but haunting memory returned. Emmy was the little girl he had witnessed that day! Long ago she had fallen into mourning for her brother and Alex had distracted himself from her mourning by pouring his energy into his baby brother's care. Recently she mourned her baby Stuart and once again Alex distracted himself, this time with his baby daughter Pauline's care.

Here was the root of their current anguish. Here was the place in which their individual wounds were hooked together like two fishhooks. Here was the clue that could restore them to life and to each other. And here was the best reason of all not to just move on, not to spiritualize away even agonizing pain, but rather to follow even the most painful feelings to their very roots — for the sake of the deepest healing, transformation, and tribute to mystery.

HERE AND NOW

CHAPTER NINE
JUST MOVE ON

Review . . .

The partner and family of a grieving person need to find the roots of their own anguish and clues about where the individual wounds hook together. If they don't, their relationships can spiral downward.

As a child, Alex saw a girl's baby brother taken from her and sacrificed for what the Emperor termed her insolence in speaking the truth. For days, the girl's cries and screams rang in his ears and his heart.

Alex, the husband of Emmy in Chapter Eight, comes to understand that an abuse of power when they were children is the root of their adult relationship challenges, evoked by the death of their son.

Consider . . .

How mysterious are the connections between us! How amazing to have the clues to the mystery, and then the mystery itself revealed. Who would have thought that what was happening between Emmy and Alex in Chapters Eight and Nine was rooted in their childhoods?

Let yourself explore two places in your own life that were perplexing, challenging, and even painful in your relationship with someone close to you. Open yourself. Welcome the clues to your mystery that might emerge now.

And Then . . .

Alex, wanting to fully restore himself to life and to his relationship with Emmy, told her he wanted to do his grief work with Aren. Alex and Aren worked together twice a week for six months to complete both the ancient and the current mourning. Emmy and Alex fully began their life and their love anew.

CHAPTER TEN

BYE-BYE, EGO

Finally, a block away from the castle, a little child's voice was heard saying, "But the Emperor has nothing on at all!" The child's father said nothing. The child's mother was silent. And the people in the crowd kept talking about the Emperor's new clothes.

"But, Mommy!" said the child, tugging on the mother's dress. "But, Daddy!" insisted the child, pulling on the father's arm. And louder still, "The Emperor has nothing on at all!" The child's mother turned away and began talking to another woman. The child's father turned around and engaged in conversation with an adolescent boy almost three times the age of his own son.

The little child stood hurt and confused, all alone in the crowd of pretending people, wanting to yell, "But the Emperor is naked! The Emperor is naked."

The child's parents turned their backs on him and walked away. The child's grandparents turned their backs on him and walked away. The child's aunts and uncles turned their backs on him and walked away. All the townspeople turned their backs on him and walked away.

The child fell to his knees in the middle of the town square, crying, "I'm right here. Don't ignore me. Don't ignore me. If we don't talk about the naked Emperor, something awful's gonna happen."

Frank grew up. He no longer remembered the day the Emperor had nothing on at all. But something haunted him. Deeply, scarily. Something definitely haunted him.

It felt ancient and it felt eerie. Frank was anxious all the time. He was a very famous writer, but no matter how well he functioned, no matter how successful his books were, something inside was gnawing at him.

Frank met a woman, Martha, and began a relationship with her. She was studying meditation and invited Frank to go with her to classes and retreats. At a loss with his own attempts to end the haunting, he embarked on a journey in search of inner peace. The meditations themselves were very helpful. They brought him information from within and helped him relax and center himself. This new practice made a great difference in his days and nights. It affected his writing, too — a new voice was developing within him.

Eventually, Frank started attending spiritual classes connected with the meditations. A well-known meditation teacher named Loren taught regularly about the need to overcome the ego. Like many meditation teachers, he insisted that his students rise above their egos.

The essence of Loren's teaching was this: If you are a true seeker, you will not let the ego make your psyche its home. In fact, you will know that any attachment to a personal self or identity will immediately create distortion in your personality.

Frank worked really hard to get rid of his ego, or as they called it in the teachings, to "transcend his ego." And he seemed to be doing a pretty good job of it for a time. But then the haunting feeling came back. He couldn't understand it. He didn't know the meaning of it. He just knew feeling haunted was part of his daily life again.

Maybe it meant he needed to put more time and energy into detaching from his ego. He spent more and more of his waking hours meditating. But the haunting remained.

Finally, Frank began to have nightmares. Nothing specific. Nothing clear. But a consistent sense of something haunting, something calling to him. Loren advised him this was a necessary stage of ridding oneself of ego. Martha concurred. Frank was a wreck. He took to his bed and slept for days — long, torturous days.

One night his dreams changed from haunting without meaning to clear communication from a wise old man who called himself Aren and said he had come to help Frank. He assured Frank of his integrity, avowing that he was a messenger from Spirit and served only Love and Truth. Frank felt hopeful, yet unsure. He turned from trying to rid himself of the haunting to asking, every day, to know the truth: *Is Aren really a manifestation of truth, or is he deception in a guise? Is my instinct to believe him really an act of self-love, or is it self-hate in disguise?* He received no direct answer. But he felt guided. It was as if two powerful hands were helping to hold him on an unmarked path so that he wouldn't stumble off.

Aren would speak to Frank in his sleep, assuring him that when he awoke he would remember everything he needed to remember in order to scribe this crucial information. Daring to trust, Frank began writing fragments of Aren's teaching in his journal day by day. Often what emerged looked like poetry.

Entry, September 20:

This approach to spirituality is ancient.
It is born of the same stuff as militarism,
simply called by spiritual names.
Its purpose: Master that
which gets in the way of your goal.
If you can't master it, conquer it.
If you can't conquer it, destroy it.
If you can't destroy it, ignore it,
get rid of it, exclude it, send it into exile.

Exile. That word. It tugged at Frank in some way that resonated with the haunting. But that is all he knew.

The entry continued . . .

And if you can't exile it,
do whatever you can to eliminate it,
even if under the guise of rising above it,
transcending it, being better than it.
I have seen many try to do this,
only to find themselves haunted
by an ego that was not rightly tended to,
only to find themselves driven by an ego
that was not properly responded to.

Haunted. There it was. What Aren was teaching resonated with Frank's experience. But he had no other words yet with which to expand upon his own experience.

Entry, September 28:

I see your way of exiling the ego
as a form of neglect under the guise of growth.
You conquer the ego as enemy;
I mature the ego as possibility.
You exile the ego as threat;
I welcome the ego as potential.
You split off from the ego as useless;
I vision the matured ego as valuable treasure,
gold yet unmined,
hope for the future.

You cast the ego off as invader;
I take the ego under my wing,
knowing I can help it grow, develop, and mature

to the point that one day it will be ready
to join with the Higher Self.
At some time the ego will be ripe
to become one with the Higher Self.
There will come a moment when
truly, not under a guise,
the ego will surrender itself,
not out of fear, but out of longing
for union with Spirit.

How beautiful this was, what was coming through him. And the particular words that tugged at him: exiling, neglect under guise, cast off. The resonance with his original haunting was becoming more and more palpable.

Entry, October 7:

Some people live
only in the outer physical world,
believing there is nothing more.
Some people believe
they are living only in the spiritual world,
in the divine world of unity,
believing there is nothing more,
believing they have transcended anything else.
But what they believe they have transcended within them
is just as active as it ever was
before they believed they had transcended it.
And it has far more power than it did before,
by virtue of their repression
and the illusion that goes with it.

So they create duality
by opting for Spirit alone,
thus splitting Spirit off from ego;
opting for the world of unity alone,
splitting it off
from the world of duality;
opting for the light alone,
splitting it off from the dark;
opting for joy alone,
splitting it off from pain;
and opting for the Self alone,
splitting it off from the self.

So they create nothing better
than those who do the exact same thing
in the opposite way.
Those who opt for ego alone,
splitting it off from Spirit;
opt for duality alone,
splitting it off from unity;
opt for darkness alone,
splitting it off from the light;
opt for pain alone,
splitting it off from joy;
opt for the self alone,
splitting it off from the Self.

I would rather be with someone
who is of the ego,
longing to learn and grow,
than with someone who believes
he has transcended the ego,

who has contempt for the ego,
and is where he believes he should be,
with no desire to include the ego
and all its energies in his journey!

'Whew! That's powerful!' thought Frank dizzily, as he read to himself what had flowed through his hand: '*But what they believe they have transcended within them is just as active as it ever was before they believed they had transcended it. And it has far more power than it did before, by virtue of their repression and the illusion that goes with it.*'

It suddenly dawned on him that trying to get rid of the ego was simply making it stronger in secret. And he now suspected what was haunting him was somehow similar.

In the midst of this profound transformation, he meditated and prayed and simply asked for help — with no word from Aren whatsoever. Then, on the night of November 12, Frank dreamed that Aren spoke directly to the teacher, Loren:

The harm you can do to yourself and those you teach is of great concern. People all over the world will put on a beautiful mask of enlightenment, fooling themselves and others with threats of fear, just like the Emperor does in the story "The Emperor's New Clothes" and with the same ultimate harm.

Still sleeping, still dreaming, Frank felt Aren take his hand and lead him. Now with the trust born of experience, he followed as Aren took him back to the town square. He watched as everyone in his young life shunned him for the purity and innocence of his truth-telling. He watched as his town exiled him for his potential, his unmined gold. He watched as he now knew what had been haunting him all his life. He watched as he knew that he was doing to his own ego what they had once done to him long, long ago.

Frank awakened feeling remorse mixed with the relief and excitement of discovery. Before going back to sleep, he wrote in his journal. First he entered his dream, then:

Dear Aren,

You are a good friend and a trusted guide. I am so grateful for your presence. You have helped me solve a life-long mystery. As part of my thanks, I will pass on what you have taught me.

Please stay in my life. I want to continue to develop our relationship forever.

With deep appreciation,

Frank

HERE AND NOW

CHAPTER TEN
BYE-BYE, EGO

Review . . .

Leaders of spiritual traditions frequently use the teachings of their path to persuade followers and practitioners to exile parts of themselves in the name of something good. Western religions try to persuade us to excise our sins, and Eastern religions try to persuade us to excise our egos.

In childhood, Frank's honesty was met by people turning their backs on him.

Frank grew up and became a famous writer. But he was anxious, haunted, all the time. A well-known spiritual teacher, Loren, taught him to "transcend" his ego. This led Frank to suppress the parts of himself that were frightening and painful.

A wise old man, Aren, a messenger from Spirit, appeared in Frank's dreams and helped Frank realize he was doing to his own ego what the townspeople had done to him long ago. Aren helped Frank heal and transform the wounds and distortions from Loren and his childhood so that his ego could become strong enough to join in union with his Higher Self and with the Divine Source.

Consider . . .

Things about ourselves that we do not meet and acknowledge will haunt us. What we try to discard will come flying back like a boomerang. No matter how we would like to get away from or disprove this truth, we cannot. These attempts have caused great damage to individuals and to our life as a world community.

❖ What part of you have you tried to throw away?

❖ Do you believe you have succeeded?

❖ What imagined consequences did you try to avoid by eliminating this aspect of yourself?

❖ Speculate about what consequences this boomerang may actually have in your life and the lives of those around you.

All the parts of yourself deserve to be met and welcomed by you. A counselor can help you, but no one else can do this for you. If you are frightened by a part of you, your task is to repair your relationship with that part and then heal the wounds and distortions in that aspect of your being. This is the work of co-creation between you and the Divine.

And Then . . .

Frank spent the next month integrating and grounding his new discovery. He stayed in communication with Aren through his dreams and even began experiencing the connection in his meditations. Eventually, he talked with Loren about his experience. Loren was open to Frank's and Aren's teachings. He talked at length with Frank, who read his journal pages aloud to Loren. Through his humility and willingness, Loren was able to restructure the way he taught his students, offering them a more organic and whole way of evolving.

CAN YOU THROW IT OVER YOUR SHOULDER LIKE A CONTINENTAL SOLDIER?

*F*inally, *a block away from the castle, a little child's voice was heard saying, "But the Emperor has nothing on at all!"*

The child's father glared at her contemptuously, hissing, "There's nothing wrong with having nothing on at all. I walk around our house like that all the time." And he removed his clothes right there in the streets of the empire.

The child turned to her mother, who looked at her with disdain. She asked her child, "How can you be concerned about the Emperor, when you have regularly seen your family like that at home?" And with that the mother took off her own clothes.

The child's older brother sneered at her and stripped to his undergarments. She insisted that she didn't like seeing him without clothes. And once she said so, she felt better until he called her "prude" and took off the rest of his clothes.

One by one the citizens of the empire took off their clothes in order to keep the Emperor from being humiliated, enraged, and vicious. Until everyone was undressed except the little child.

She didn't like seeing everybody without anything on at all. She didn't want to take off her own clothes. But she also didn't want to be humiliated for disliking what the others were doing and for being different

from everyone else. She stood in her clothes, holding her arms around her-
self, frozen in her tracks.

Alice grew up. She no longer remembered the day the Emperor had
nothing on at all.

She was uncomfortable in her body, but she couldn't have put it into
words or known why. In her teens she attempted to play sports, but she
couldn't run or jump or aim or catch. She tried dancing but quickly
became discouraged by her awkwardness. So Alice became an artist, a tal-
ented one at that. And although she wasn't yet aware of it, she painted
picture after picture from the perspective of a child frozen in her tracks,
seeing clearly but unable to move.

Over the years, her sedentary way of life took a toll on her back and
neck. Alice found herself in pain every single day. She tried chiropractic,
acupuncture, Reiki, Rolfing, massage, and Pilates. Although she'd heard
these modalities had helped other people, none of them helped her long-
term. Finally she discovered a relatively new bodywork, Body Bright, a
form of healing that had been developed in Colorado by a team of men
and women led by Harold Bright.

Alice contacted a Bright practitioner, a trim, red-headed, middle-
aged woman named Reena. Taking care to gather the information she
needed in order to feel safe and to proceed, Alice included in her questions, "Is the Bright work done on clients who are clothed or
unclothed?" The practitioner explained that the work was done with
clients fully clothed. With all her questions answered, Alice began treatments. Within eight weeks, there was a significant change in her body.
The constant pain dissolved and she found herself with only periodic
hurts and aches. She was thrilled and so awed by this work, she wanted
to train to do it for others.

It was possible for Alice to be trained very quickly. It took only two
three-day weekends for her to learn the basics and begin practicing. She
would never have taken this path, given her lack of knowledge in the

field of bodywork, but for the assurances she received that the Bright technique could cause no harm.

With great expectations, Alice signed up for the course. She attended the first day and was doing fine until the instructor, Archer, prepared to demonstrate basic strokes on someone. First he modeled the technique on a man, a Bright practitioner who came into the room wearing only a jock strap and a blue tee shirt emblazoned with the words Body Bright. Once on the table, the man removed his tee shirt.

The contrast between what she had been told and experienced with Reena, remaining fully clothed, and what she was witnessing in the class, the partial nudity, was unexpected and distressing.

Alice felt frozen and was afraid soon everyone would be asked to take off his or her clothing. She didn't want them to remove their clothes. She didn't want to take off her own clothes. But she also dreaded being humiliated for not liking what the others were doing and for not joining them. The degree of agitation she felt was mysterious to her, but she didn't have time to explore it for herself. Archer had begun to teach the first series of basic strokes and had promised he would teach at a steady clip.

Somehow she over-rode the frozenness enough to takes notes and to look like she was doing fine. She hung in there throughout the next half hour. But then Archer announced that it was time for the students to practice. A team of certified Body Bright workers entered the room, dressed in only their Body Bright tee shirts and briefs. Alice gasped as she realized that one of these was Reena, her own bodyworker, and that the students were expected to practice on the nearly naked professionals. Reena came over to Alice's group, stretched out on the table, and took off her shirt.

For Alice, to see her practitioner's bare breasts breached an invisible boundary and shattered the safety that good boundaries provide. It modeled an unsafe standard for practicing here in class and also out in the world.

After an hour's practice session, the professionals left, the class took a short break, and when they returned, the students were to practice on each other. They all began disrobing.

Alice froze again. She didn't want to touch anyone's bare body. She did not want anyone touching her bare skin. In fact, with the breaching of that boundary, the atmosphere of the whole workshop had begun to feel unsafe. So now she didn't want anyone to touch her even on top of her clothes. She was amazed at the courage she was able to muster to talk to Archer about this. They solved the problem by having Alice simply observe for most of the session and practice on Archer through his tee shirt for the last 15 minutes.

Alice made it through the training with great strain on her body, mind, heart, and soul. She stayed focused on the work and disconnected from her feelings during the day. At night she rewrote her notes, practiced on her pillow, and then cried herself to sleep, not really understanding what was being triggered for her.

At the end of the training, Archer suggested they go home and practice on everyone they knew — family, friends, and clients alike. Alice gave free sessions to her art colleagues and appropriate friends, even though Archer had given the okay for them to charge people. She felt uncomfortable about charging fees, having no training or credentials as a therapist or massage therapist and having just begun her training as a Bright therapist.

Archer made himself available to everyone for phone consultations, and Alice took him up on his offer a number of times over the next weeks. At first she felt she was doing well, and people were experiencing the benefits of their sessions with her. But two months into her practicing, feeling her work was becoming stagnant, she asked Archer if she could do a day's worth of practice with him. She was committed to becoming the best Body Bright practitioner she could possibly be. Alice sensed that if she could practice on Archer again, he would be able to tell, by experiencing her work, whether she was doing it accurately and how he might help her improve.

They agreed on time, place, and fee. Alice was hopeful about the prospect of mastering this technique in a way that could really be of service to people. She also hoped her growing proficiency could make it possible for her to someday, in good conscience, charge a fee. The practice day came. As she walked into Archer's treatment room, Alice was surprised at how tall he seemed in this context. Even though she had practiced on him, she hadn't realized his stature in the group setting. But his brown wavy hair, neatly trimmed beard, and dark piercing eyes were the same.

She worked well with Archer, who was kind and patient with her. She left at the end of the day re-inspired in her work.

For the next few months, Alice's Bright practice was thrilling. People had encouraging responses to her treatments in relatively few sessions. She allowed each success to enliven her work while continuing the phone consultations with Archer.

In the meantime, she began having unpleasant dreams, vaguely familiar, echoes of something she couldn't quite remember.

At first she could recall only fragments: A sense of people with no clothing, a sense of being uncomfortable, a sense of people ridiculing her for her discomfort. She couldn't identify any experience like that other than the Bright training class. But in some as-yet-unexplainable way, the dreams felt different from the training.

She prayed to understand the source of these dreams. Finally, one night, Alice dreamed the entire experience. When she awakened, she realized this was not merely a dream, but a memory from long, long ago when the Emperor and the whole town — except she herself — had nothing on at all. She was both pleased to have this knowledge and shaken by what she now knew.

Having once worked with a psychoanalyst for many years, Alice made an appointment and took the dream-memory to him. He helped her discern what in her life was simply evoking this memory and what in her life was of real here-and-now concern.

As she continued giving Bright sessions, Alice found herself eager to schedule another practice day with Archer. She made the appointment with him. Having recovered the dream-memory, she wanted to share it with Archer. This would help him understand her behavior in the class and would perhaps lead him to reconsider nudity in his teaching workshops. After all, how many others had histories of their own that he couldn't possibly know, histories that made an unsafe environment even more damaging? With this awareness he could also better honor her boundaries and take his responsibility as a teacher to new levels.

"It's an honor, Alice," Archer said warmly, "that you would trust me, given your history." He hesitated an instant and then said casually, "Let's hope I'm not careless with your trust."

Alice was scared about the "careless" part. It made her stomach turn to think he might be careless, yet she had experienced only respect from him so far. And although she had a good imagination, she couldn't picture how he could be careless with her in this context.

Instead of the bathing suit he had worn in the first practice session, this time Archer had on a pair of boxer undershorts. About half-way into the session, just as she had done the first time they had worked together, Alice told him she would leave the room to give him privacy while he turned over from his belly to his back.

When she returned and carefully pulled the sheet aside to work on his thigh, Archer's penis was sticking out of his boxers. She was stunned and frozen. It would be one thing if this happened with a client, but Archer wasn't a client. He was her teacher.

It was as though she moved to another part of her being, leaving the frozen part where it was, and continued the practice on automatic pilot. Reflexively, she covered him with the sheet and went on to the next procedure. She went all through the afternoon in this manner.

Alice paid Archer and thanked him. They said goodbye. She stayed on autopilot for a few hours, and only came out that night while taking a shower. As the frozenness melted under the hot water, she knew she would have to talk with Archer about this. To do so would be frightening, but given her experiences with him so far, she hoped they could repair the damage to her trust and to their working relationship.

At first, Archer expressed surprise and remorse. "Oh, I'm sorry. I don't know how it happened. I was trying. I guess that type of men's underwear — it can happen."

He coughed and then continued, "I'm not one to look at things so deeply. Self-analysis is not my thing. Assessing if my action or lack of action caused something is too involved for me. I guess there was something more I could have done to prevent what happened. At some level, it must be my fault. I hope I can earn your trust back, Alice."

Alice was amazed. Alice was grateful. She had dared to be open, honest, and vulnerable with good results. She had not noticed that this positive outcome was sabotaged already. The clue was Archer's language. No wonder the undermining was certain even as he spoke. He claimed fault rather than responsibility. Fault and blame are of the same family. They imply someone is bad. No one can sustain them. They are like a poison you have to spit out. On the other hand, on the deepest levels of our being, we hunger for responsibility and accountability which do *not* make someone bad.

Nevertheless, Alice imagined that his response now allowed repair, resolution, and a continuing relationship. Not so fast! In an instant, without any apparent cause, he switched his tone, becoming defensive, even attacking.

"Listen, Alice, what happened was purely an accident. I was being careful. It was simply an unfortunate occurrence. Your discomfort with it is your problem."

Alice's heart sank. She turned away, silent for a time, and then turned back to Archer.

"This doesn't have to do with just me, Archer. All of us, including practitioners, have unconscious stuff we don't remember about nakedness. And this is the reason you weren't even aware you were leaving yourself hanging out of your boxers. As long as you continue to practice that way . . . even if I practiced that way, I would leave myself and my clients vulnerable. We have no awareness of what is likely to open in a person when he or she is exposed to nudity.

"It's not your fault. I believe you didn't do it consciously and on purpose. But yes! It is your responsibility because you have a way of practicing that is bound to lead to such an outcome. And somehow you knew unconsciously 'cause you said to me, 'Let's hope I'm not careless with your trust.'"

Archer shrugged his shoulders, sighed, "Oh, well," and asked Alice offhandedly if she would like to schedule another practice session.

Alice saw what was happening through her own artist-eyes: If Archer were an artist and painted warped pictures, instead of admitting his vision was distorted, he would justify the warped paintings by pretending they were examples of an exotic style of art. Critiquing his art would do no good unless he could acknowledge the source of the problem was his distorted eyesight.

With this realization, Alice knew it would be fruitless to continue with Archer, but the experience still hurt. It duplicated the ancient memory that had returned in her dreams, which was her part to heal; but it also revealed something about the limitations of this man, perhaps other bodywork teachers, the Body Bright standards, and certainly any system of bodywork that naively encourages nudity.

A very competent woman, Alice did what she could on her own, stretching herself only as far as felt safe. She sought further training with a different Bright teacher, a woman who was beginning a small practice group for certified Body Bright workers. In spite of her previous experiences, Alice was again shocked when her new teacher stripped practically naked at the group's first meeting.

Alice wrote to Arlene Sussex, head of the Body Bright Foundation, at its world headquarters in Boston, wanting to inform her of the problems within the ranks so they could be resolved. On a weekend art excursion to the Boston area, Alice finally met with Ms. Sussex.

Alice felt that Arlene was investigating the situation with half an ear, half a heart, and an intention to defend her teachers. How disappointing! Not only did the practitioners and teachers Alice had met lack awareness of what happens in a room where people are working on other people's bodies, but the same lack of consciousness existed in the organization's leader.

Alice explained to Arlene, "Whether I am sculpting or painting someone's likeness or doing Bright work with a client, to me each body is sacred in itself. I attune to the body and to the whole sacred being with respect. This has not been my experience with the Bright trainers or practitioners."

Arlene snapped back, "They're just bodies. You have to learn to respond to them that way or you'll get yourself into trouble."

"I could never do that," moaned Alice. "And what kind of trouble are you talking about? I think the Bright organization and its members are already in trouble. The mask of enlightenment about nakedness — their own and that of others — leads them, their trainees, and their clients down a dangerous path. A path of which they don't seem to be aware. And worse, they don't seem to want the awareness."

"So what! They're only doing bodywork," interjected Arlene.

"My sense, Arlene, is that some of the people at trainings are being used and objectified; some are being stimulated and turned on; and those with an unconscious tendency to abuse their power as caregivers are being tempted to violate and damage others, whether in blatant or subtle ways. What I have seen is not a safe environment in which to train people to work with others. It's not safe for the trainees, their clients, or their future students. The trainees will carry the modeling of the Body Bright teachers within them, both the conscious practice and the underlying tone and motivation, and do the same thing with others.

"Profound changes need to be made at an organizational level to come into alignment with safety and ethics," finished Alice.

Arlene replied simply and curtly, "What you are saying might be more ethical and safe, my dear, but not practical. It would take revamping of our whole system of teaching, which is very effective. There is no need to change our way of working."

Alice experienced physical revulsion at this lack of integrity. She was also disappointed and heartbroken. She had such appreciation for the Bright technique, but she could not stay involved with an organization that was unsafe, unconscious, and without any intention to change — even if it meant she could not continue to learn the treatments. At the same time, Alice felt so good about having spoken up again, as she once had long, long ago. It was as though that terrible memory was the fairy-tale straw spun into gold.

Still, she wanted to talk about this with someone she trusted, someone who could truly comprehend the depth of meaning and concern in the situation. She called her friend, Aren, a massage therapist and teacher of massage at a reputable school in the area. Fortunately, Aren was free, and they agreed to meet for dinner in half an hour.

At the restaurant, they began a soulful conversation about Alice's experiences with the Bright organization. Aren listened quietly as Alice shared.

With the full story told, Aren began, "Dear friend, you are wise to see this issue and courageous to address it. Sadly, there is so much unconsciousness in our bodywork field. Only the most sensitive people realize the seriousness of touch. We never know what will open up in a person's body and psyche when we touch them. Or even when they watch someone else being touched. Even when someone has done a tremendous amount of work in her soul journey, ancient wounds held in the body can erupt into consciousness in a way that perhaps no other modality can cause. The bodyworker needs to understand this. The only way he or she can do that is to have done enough personal work to know what is in his or her own body, mind, heart, and soul.

"You instinctively knew, Alice, that there was something not on target to have the Bright work learned so quickly. By your unfortunate experience, you have discovered for yourself there is more to doing safe bodywork than simply the mechanics of a treatment method. Your own body's physical revulsion to the conversation with Arlene informed you of the harm that comes when someone in a position of power has an intention to stay unconscious. Arlene did this when she claimed, as though it were justified . . . what did she say again?"

Alice remembered clearly. "'What you are saying might be more ethical and safe, my dear, but not practical.'"

"Yes," Aren nodded, "and Archer did the same when he refused to take responsibility for his sexual self."

Alice giggled, "I don't know why I thought of this but there's a song I learned from nuns in summer day camp during the 1950's. It goes like this:

Do your ears hang low?
Do they wobble to and fro?
Can you tie 'em in a knot?
Can you tie 'em in a bow?
Can you throw 'em over your shoulder
Like a continental soldier?
Do your ears hang low?"

Chuckling, Aren told Alice the original version of the song, in which the word "balls" had not been replaced by "ears."

As their laughter died down, Aren continued, "Actually Alice, there's a story they tell in Jungian circles about a man who has a penis twelve feet long. It is so long, in fact, that he goes through his life wearing it thrown over his shoulder. What that means, however, is that his penis does whatever it does behind his back, where he has no consciousness of its activity or impact, and so feels no need to take responsibility for the results."

Alice laughed, "What a great way to describe what I have met in the Body Bright organization!"

"Yes, Alice. And sadly, it will take generations to set this one right. Yet think of it this way: When somebody like you takes inner and outer action as you have, it is not too dramatic to say you are helping humanity evolve. Everything each of us can do in our own development and that of others will be a contribution. I am personally grateful for your contribution. Your involvement with the Bright organization, as painful as it was, has helped you come a long way from being frozen in your tracks."

Alice answered thoughtfully. "Thank you for your recognition of the importance of my small and not-so-small contribution, Aren."

Aren smiled and nodded appreciatively at her way of naming the paradox.

Alice smiled and nodded with him, then went on. "Aren, I don't want to live the rest of my life rigid with fear when I need to disrobe or frozen in my tracks when I see somebody with nothing on at all. Can you recommend someone who is both a therapist and a massage therapist, who knows and honors the profound effect of touch on a person's body, heart, mind, and soul, and who can help me heal these things?"

"I sure can, Alice." Aren immediately had a suggestion. "The dean of my massage school fits your description to a T. She's well-trained in both fields, seasoned in her art, continues to do her own personal work and to receive training and supervision, and has a depth of understanding, compassion, and integrity that places her with the best therapists in both fields. I think she may be just the right person for you," he finished as he wrote the woman's name and phone number.

"Thank you so much, Aren." Alice took the paper and put it in her pocket. "You are a dear friend." And the two continued their dinner in lively conversation.

HERE AND NOW

CHAPTER ELEVEN
CAN YOU THROW IT OVER YOUR SHOULDER LIKE A CONTINENTAL SOLDIER?

Review . . .

Some practitioners in energy and bodywork fields such as massage, Reiki, and other forms of hands-on healing violate the sacredness of the body under a multiplicity of disguised motives. They are often unaware what will open up in a person's body and psyche and lack adequate training to truly help with the opening that occurs.

As a child, Alice did not like seeing her parents and people in the town square take off their clothes.

Alice grew up uncomfortable, almost frozen, in her body. An artist and student of bodywork, she considered each body sacred, a view the leader and teachers of her training institute demeaned. They also pooh-poohed her search for ethical and responsible practice and teaching.

Alice's friend Aren, a massage therapist and teacher, supported Alice in her sacred healing. With his encouragement and her commitment, she will be able to restore the parts of her body that were frozen.

Consider . . .

Our bodies are sacred, just like every other aspect of our beings. Yet most of us have not healed our personal and our communal wounds sufficiently to truly treat our bodies and those of others with reverence.

Instead, under a multiplicity of disguised motives, bodies are unclothed, observed, touched, and more — in ways that turn out to be harmful. Under the guise of being in vogue, progressive, mature. Under the guise of teaching and learning. Under the guise of healing. Under the guise of caretaking. Under the guise of mothering and fathering. Under the guise of play. Under the guise of love. Even under the guise of holiness!

❖ How have you experienced irreverence or mistreatment of your body?

❖ What disguises of irreverent motivations can you now see through?

And Then . . .

Alice called the woman to whom Aren had referred her and began work with her the next week. She was amazed and dismayed at the length of time it took her to thaw herself and dissolve her fear. Nevertheless, she was as fierce in her commitment to herself as she had been in her commitment to holding the Body Bright organization accountable.

Archer and the Body Bright teachers continued to practice and teach their bodywork method in their practical but unsafe and unethical ways. Thousands of unsuspecting people all over the world went to them for healing and training.

PLAYING WITH SEXUAL ENERGY IS PLAYING WITH FIRE

inally, a block away from the castle, a little child's voice was heard saying, "But the Emperor has nothing on at all!"

The child's father whispered, "The better to practice sacred rites."

The child's uncle whispered, "The better to practice sacred rites."

And the child's grandfather whispered, "The better to practice sacred rites." The men all had a hungry feeling to their whispers, which the child did not understand.

The child's grandmother said, "It is time to introduce you, then, to sacred rites."

The child's aunt joined in, "It is time, little one, for you to see sacred rites."

The child's mother took her hand, telling her, "Since you see what is, child, it is time to teach you sacred rites." Intertwined with what seemed to be holy words was, on the one hand, a flat matter-of-factness, and on the other, a deep sadness.

The child had no idea what was happening. She merely had seen that the Emperor had nothing on at all and had said so. The women took her into the palace. They walked her into the sacred rites chambers. Everyone in the chamber really had nothing on at all, men and women alike.

What was going on here? Whatever it was turned her stomach, but she didn't know why or what it meant.

People were all entwined with one another, breathing deeply and making sounds. The Emperor was there, going from one woman to the next. The little girl was curious and felt like throwing up at the same time.

Her kinswomen took her into a special chamber where little girls were being bathed, rubbed with aromatic oils, and wrapped in special cloth, this time real cloth — not that of the pretend tailors.

The Emperor came to the door of the room and said, "Bring me for sacred rites the one who saw I had nothing on at all." The child's grandmother, aunt, and mother escorted her into the Emperor's personal sacred rites room, then left her all alone with him.

He began by saying to her, "Only special little girls get to learn the sacred rites that are usually saved for women. You have wisdom and courage beyond your years. As a result, you spoke out today, proving yourself to be a special little girl.

"You must follow my every instruction if you want to be initiated as a special little girl and be able to connect not only with me but also with the gods all around us."

The child obeyed the Emperor's every instruction that day and learned the sacred rites.

Sally grew up. For a young woman in her 20's, she was wise, courageous, and precocious — ripened before her time. She no longer remembered the day the Emperor had nothing on at all.

She became a staff member at a modern retreat center. One of her staff benefits was to attend center workshops of interest to her. A teacher came one weekend to teach tantra — a sacred spiritual practice through which people use sexual experience to connect with the Divine. Sally was inexplicably drawn to the workshop.

The teacher taught about tantra and then told the students that tantra is not something to learn about but, rather, a practice to experience. She taught them specific tantric exercises and encouraged them to discover the intentions and meanings of each by entering into it. Sally's stomach turned but she didn't know why or what it meant. She listened and watched intently, finding herself curious and yet nauseous at the same time. The instructor told them how special each of them was and how precious was this opportunity for them to be initiated into the sacred tantric practices. Sally listened, and it all felt strangely familiar.

At each day's end, the leader suggested the participants practice with their friends in preparation for the next day. And Sally did. She practiced the first exercise with her staff peer, Jon; the second exercise with another participant in the workshop, Phil; and the third exercise with her friend, Marco. She felt compelled to follow the teacher's instructions.

The workshop ended and Sally moved back into her daily schedule with one addition: She continued to set times during each day for practicing tantra with her friends at the center.

The following week, Sally attended another event, this one led by a spiritual teacher named Mita.

When Mita invited participants to explore a personal issue of their choice, Sally was the first to come forward. She explored how she held herself back in the sexual relationship with her boyfriend. With Mita's guidance, through a deep and honest journey into her feelings, Sally discovered how she habitually split herself while being intimate with him: Her young self from her adult self; her frightened self from her passionate self; her out-of-body self from her embodied self. She realized that she pushed away any feelings that emerged in order to keep "having sex." She also discovered how she split herself in another way: one part practicing tantra with her friends; another part entering into an intimate relationship with her boyfriend.

With Mita's help, Sally realized that at some prior time she had made a decision to manage her sexuality and her life force in this way. Within the intensity of this feeling experience, she birthed a new decision. She would bring everything to her sexual experience with her lover. This work was rich and beautiful. The entire group was moved. When Mita invited people to share, both the men and the women acknowledged how they had been affected by Sally's work. A number of them felt moved, as a result, to volunteer to explore their own sexuality in a respectful, boundaried, and safe way.

Just as Mita began to work with another woman, Sally interjected that she had one more thing she needed to say. She would need to leave this session early to practice tantra with a friend before lunch.

Mita asked for more information, and the whole story about the tantra workshop came out. Others in the workshop nodded their heads as Sally filled in the picture, letting Mita know that many of these young men and women had attended last week's workshop.

Mita was concerned on many levels, the foremost of which was Sally's well-being, followed by that of the other members of the group and of the group as an entity. "Your sexual energy individually and communally has been called out by the tantra workshop. Sexual energy is a very powerful energy. It is like fire. It is fire. And like fire, or any energy, it can be well used, consciously, in the service of truth and love and with everyone's best interests at heart. It can also be misused and abused, unconsciously or willfully, even under the guise of something healthy and sacred. I am troubled about the way you seem to understand the truly sacred tantric teachings. Either they were mistaught last week or have been misunderstood and misinterpreted.

"Those of you who were at the workshop may have felt you had permission to explore your sexuality in a time and manner that may not be good for you. It may be easy to be sexual with someone you won't see again for a long time; and you all are leaving the center at the end of the season, two weeks from now. Some people find it easier to let go sexually with an acquaintance than with someone with whom they share deep intimacy. For example, Sally, it is intriguing that you can experiment with men here at the center, yet you hold back with your boyfriend. Finally, none of you seem to be considering whether it is in your best interest, or even safe, to be sexual with other staff members here at the center."

Sally angrily shot back at Mita. "Those are very strong words for a workshop leader to utter! I have a right to make my own choices."

Mita responded open-heartedly. "You are right, Sally. My statement was strong. And you do have a right to your own choices. Each of us has free will, and I honor your right and need to exercise your free will.

"At the same time, I have seen again and again the harm that can come of a situation which calls out sexual energy in a group without a commitment to attune to each individual in the process. I've seen this happen in therapeutic and spiritual groups, where people were skinny-dipping, doing group massage in the nude, exploring body images by standing naked before mirrors, doing sacred rituals at a river, or even participating in a sweat lodge. I've known it to happen in groups with men and women together and also in groups of women only or men only.

"For example, you said at the beginning of your work today that you believe you were sexually abused, although you don't have a specific tangible memory yet. In my experience, Sally, that is exactly one of the wounds that can make dangerous an experience like last week's tantra workshop. Sexual abuse leaves people vulnerable in ways that evade consciousness until years into their healing.

"I've worked with people who had been in situations like the one last week, carrying out the tasks assigned for what seemed to them Higher Self reasons. They trusted the leader, wanted to be closer to the Divine Source, longed to heal their sexual wounds; but it turned out in the end that these reasons blinded them to other aspects of what was occurring. As a result, days or weeks, months or years later, they discovered with horror that they felt betrayed and violated, both by the leader and by themselves. Do you understand?" Mita asked, looking around the room and then at Sally. Everyone in the room nodded.

And then Sally replied, "Yes," half attentively, half grudgingly.

"The truth," Mita continued, "is that many of us may be wounded sexually, men and women alike. We may have been wounded by a parent, another relative, or some person who violated our sacred body and our sacred sexual energy in our personal life. Or we may have been wounded by the evolving but grossly twisted and distorted sexual energy in our culture. Many of us, maybe even most of us, may be sexually wounded. And this wound is screaming to be healed.

"The sexual wound is calling to be healed in our bodies, hearts, and souls, in our waking lives and our dream lives, and in our relationships. It is demanding to be healed through last week's workshop. It is insisting on being healed through the sexual scandals our political and religious leaders are facing month after month. These are mirrors of our individual and cultural distortions of sexuality.

"Sexual abuse all over the world is criminalized. That it is also ritualized and normalized is a sign of how urgently this misuse of power needs healing. Do you see, Sally, so many men and women misinterpret all intimacy as sexual just because they feel isolated and hungry to be held? This is another symptom of how imperative it is that we be participants and co-creators in the healing of our sexual energy."

Sally took a deep breath. "Even though I may want my right to choose, and even though I may rail at you for trying to restrict me, I really want to do what is truth for me in my journey. And I don't want to misuse anything in that process."

"That's beautiful, Sally." Mita smiled.

Sally smiled back, then her face became troubled. "There's one more thing, Mita. This all has seemed strangely compelling to me and mysteriously familiar. I don't know what to make of it."

"What specifically is familiar, Sally?" asked Mita.

"Well, first it felt like I was being taken to the tantra workshop by something that was not in my control. Then, being told that because I am special, I have the honor of learning these sacred sexual rites. Being taught to practice these rites with many people. And a feeling in my body of curiosity and excitement mixed with nausea and 'the creeps.'"

"Are you open to trying something to see if we can solve the mystery, Sally?" asked Mita.

"Yes, Mita, as long as we can stop if I want to."

"Of course, Sally. All you have to do is say 'Stop, Mita,' and I will stop in a heartbeat! You need to say my name, because otherwise I will think you are simply saying 'Stop' as part of your expression in the exploration."

"That feels safe enough, Mita."

"So, Sally, in a moment I will ask you to close your eyes and then I will guide you inside yourself to find if there is another time in your soul's journey that was somehow similar to your journey last week. Shall we begin?"

"Okay."

"Now, Sally, close your eyes and breathe. Let each breath be a little bit deeper than the one before it. Let your breathing take on a life of its own. And now relax on the river of your breath, which is Spirit, allowing it to take you into your own underground labyrinths, carrying you steadily and consistently to your center — that place within where your human self and your Divine Self are one.

"When you arrive at the center, Sally, let yourself rest there and then ask to be carried to any point in your soul's journey that will shed light and healing on this past week's experiences. Now let go as I count you back from the present moment to whatever answer is available to you at this time.

"Ten. Nine. Eight. Seven . . . Two. One. And zero. Now take the time to sense in all ways where you are and what is occurring. When you are ready, tell me about it."

And, in the voice of a five-year-old child, Sally told the whole story, from the moment she first saw the Emperor had nothing on at all to the moment he initiated her into the sacred rites. When the story had been told, Sally pushed against the air as if fending off an adversary, screaming,

"No! No! No!" first as a young girl and then as her womanly self. As the waves of feeling subsided and her breathing evened out, she crawled over to Mita, laid her head in Mita's lap, and began weeping anew.

With one hand behind Sally's heart and the other on the crown of her head, Mita held Sally literally and figuratively. After a few minutes, Sally looked up at Mita and said, "It is amazing, Mita. I thought I was so conscious. And I had no idea how profoundly my childhood experience was affecting me and driving my life."

"How wonderful that you have been open to finding the truth beneath the surface, Sally. How wonderful that we could all together co-create one small step toward the healing of sexuality in your life and in our world."

HERE AND NOW

PLAYING WITH SEXUAL ENERGY
IS PLAYING WITH FIRE

Review . . .

Leaders with distortions about sexuality and power communicate them to their students. Those who were wounded sexually by a parent, a relative, or some person who violated their sacred body and sacred sexual energy are most vulnerable. However, we are all vulnerable.

When Sally was a child, her father, mother, and grandparents introduced her to the world of sexual encounter under the guise of sacred rites.

Sally grew up and she attended a workshop on tantra — a spiritual practice through which people use sexual experience to connect with the Divine. However, her teacher at the spiritual center failed to communicate the great power of sexual energy and the responsibility to use that power well.

As a result, the students were left to misuse their sexual power in ways destructive to themselves and to each other. Sally met Mita, a spiritual teacher at the same center. Mita guided Sally on an inner journey. Sally opened to finding the truth about the abuse in her childhood and took a step toward healing the distorted sexuality in her life and in the world.

Consider . . .

It is up to people in positions of authority to make sure they commit to resolving any distortions of thoughts, feelings, attitudes, and visions about power. Only then can they be trusted to use the power that comes with leadership. If the leader fails to do the necessary work to assure the right use of power, then it is up to those in the community to hold the leader accountable and to protect themselves and each other.

Too often, however, the members of the community — whether as large as the world community or as small as the family community — are unable or unwilling to stand up in the face of the misuse of power. Instead, they collude with the leader and compound the damage, as a result.

So much in our world that is injurious could not happen without the collusion of others. Whether conscious or unconscious, vocal or tacit, complicity creates fertile ground for the misuse of power and the damage that comes of it.

Cult leaders cannot wreak their havoc without those who idealize and submit to them and others who ignore their activities. Hitler could not have destroyed as he did without the people who colluded with him, actively and passively alike. Political leaders cannot pull the wool over the eyes of their constituents unless their constituents are somehow invested in the scam.

In Sally's childhood, her whole family colluded with the Emperor's supposed sacred rites. Her father, uncle, and grandfather encouraged her by saying, "The better to practice sacred rites." But even more harmful, her mother, aunt, and grandmother, weaving together what seemed like holy words, matter-of-factness, and sadness, led Sally into the Emperor's bed chambers to be abused by him, just as each of them had once been led long, long ago.

In her adulthood, Sally learned tantra from a teacher who apparently neglected to communicate that sexual energy is fire and needs to be handled with great care. As a result of this omission, the students mishandled their sexual fire, playing with it in damaging ways.

❖ All of us have dealings with people in authority. Have you ever felt that someone who had authority over you was misusing that power?

❖ Who were the people in your community at that time who might have said or done something on your behalf and did not?

❖ Where in your life have you experienced abusive power being aided by neglect, silence, or feigned agreement?

And Then . . .

Sally, faced with her new awareness, longed for more consciousness and more healing of her wounded sexuality. Because of the connection she had made with Mita, Sally asked Mita to work with her. With every session, Sally connected more deeply with herself, and as a result she was more able to connect with her boyfriend in all areas of their life together.

THERE'S ONLY ONE
AUTHORITY HERE, AND I'M IT

*F*inally, a block away from the castle, a little child's voice was heard saying, "But the Emperor has nothing on at all!"

"What did you say?" asked a woman standing nearby.

"But the Emperor has nothing on at all!" replied the child.

"I can't hear you. Say it again!" urged a man behind the child.

"But the Emperor has nothing on at all!" repeated the child.

"Say it loud enough for the whole village to hear you," encouraged the little boy's friend, the baker, thinking if anyone could safely say it, a child could.

"But the Emperor has nothing on at all!" boomed the child one more time.

"Who said that?" roared the Emperor's soldiers.

"He did! He did! He did!" pointed all the citizens, who liked knowing the truth but wanted no responsibility for it.

Again, "Who said that?"

And again, "He did. He did." The people pointed frantically, even the baker, and opened a path through the crowd straight to the child.

"What did you say?" asked the commander of the army, standing right before the child.

"But the Emperor has nothing on at all!" responded the child truthfully.

And the Emperor's soldiers dragged the little boy to the gallows, to teach the townspeople a lesson.

And so they did. Everyone now knew the truth. Everyone knew the Emperor had no clothes on at all. And everyone now knew for certain that one dared not say the truth aloud. It was too dangerous.

Scarcely anyone knew that the soldiers had not actually executed the little boy. As long as everyone believed they had, it was all the same — the lesson had been learned. Even those who knew had no more trouble pretending the boy had been executed than they had pretending the Emperor was wearing splendid clothing.

Peter grew up. He no longer remembered the day the Emperor had nothing on at all. Recently retired from a 43-year career as an elementary school teacher, Peter now treasured devoting his talents to serving his town as a volunteer in the schools, in the hospital, and wherever else he was needed.

Despite ongoing involvement with many people, Peter felt alone. He longed for community — a community of truth and love where people could be both equals and leaders at the same time. A community that joined the spiritual with the ordinary, where people could be close with each other and trust that everyone would be held sacred. Peter gave and led and kept looking for such a community.

At last! He thought he had found it. A spiritual community encircling a lake that claimed it believed in living from the inside out and appeared to know the healing power of feelings. Could this be his dream come true?

Peter, filled with care, slowly, cautiously began to explore the community and follow its path. He went to several workshops. His heart leapt with excitement. He began to work with a community spiritual mentor. He joined the monthly Community Learning Program. He felt guided by Spirit. His soul felt at home at last.

For a year Peter grew and grew and not only practiced, but also lived what he was being taught. A longstanding hunger within him was being fed. He felt full and satisfied. He felt he was in heaven on earth.

Because this was such a joyous venture for Peter, he really was a model student. He was truthful, real, and undefended. He owned both his "yes" and his "no" — the better to clear the pathway to act on his "yes." He took responsibility for his part in any interaction.

One day Peter acknowledged his own part in a tension with a fellow community member, expecting the other person to do likewise. When the other person sat in silence, shaking her head in denial, Peter also described her part. Several others in the group egged Peter on. "You tell 'er, Peter. Enough of it always being only one person's issues. Let everyone look at their responsibility here."

Buoyed by their support, when the woman continued shaking her head, Peter repeated what he had said.

The community spiritual leader hastened over, asking, "What is going on here?"

Peter said, "We are asking this woman to own her responsibility for helping to create a tense situation."

One man started yelling at Peter to speak only for himself. Another reminded him in a condescending manner to use his "I-statements." Someone else accused him of being in his lower self. And yet another community member pushed at him to take the log out of his own eye before he expects her to look at herself.

Peter was stunned. He didn't know what had hit him. But he knew he was grievously wounded.

Peter tried turning to his friends. All those who had previously encouraged him silently joined with the authorities to protect their own skins. He turned to his mentor.

His teacher would have nothing to do with him, instead lapping up the praise of the community authorities in an effort to keep herself safe.

In great despair, Peter packed his suitcase, got in his car, and left. He wept as he drove away from the lake and onto the local roads.

Suddenly he was taken aback by a police car passing him with lights flashing, signaling him to pull over. Once his car was stopped, Peter rested his head against the steering wheel, feeling weak with desolation. The policeman found him sobbing uncontrollably when he got to the car.

"Whoa! Man. What's wrong here, Pops?" asked the policeman.

"You wouldn't understand," Peter whimpered the best he could through his tears.

"Here ya go. Try me," the officer replied, opening the door and gently drawing Peter out of the car.

"Please," said Peter. "Just give me the ticket and let me go home by myself."

"Oh, no ya don't," said Officer Aren. "We're gonna have a talk here before I put ya back in that car."

The officer took Peter to the side of the road, overlooking a river. Peter said, "I can't," curled up on the riverbank, and felt as though he were falling into a chasm echoing with the cries of his heart.

"Oh, my God, Pops. What's happened to ya?" At a loss, the officer found himself asking this rhetorical question as an expression of his kindness and as a way to let Peter know he was there and he cared. He put his hand on the back of Peter's neck and sat with him in his agony.

After they'd sat on the riverbank for at least a half hour, Officer Aren received a radio page. Not wanting to leave Peter alone, he pulled out his cell phone, called the station, and announced to the policeman on the other end, "I'm going off duty for a while. I've got a bit o' God's work to do now." He put the phone away and resumed his vigil with Peter.

Peter heard what Officer Aren had done and said. And although it made no sense to him, he was deeply moved.

The two remained there together for some hours, neither aware of how long, and neither caring. At times Peter felt the policeman's hand on his neck or shoulder; at times he heard the officer's breathing; at other times there was silence; and at still others, Peter thought he heard this kind patrolman praying.

Finally, as Peter started to breathe in an easy, open rhythm, the policeman leaned toward him and said, "I'm Officer Aren. My friends call me

Aren. It seems ya've had a rough time of it. By the sound of it, I would venture a guess that ya've just had an experience that opened up somethin' from yer childhood."

"What!" responded Peter. "I thought you were a policeman, not a therapist."

"Yes, Pops, I am on the police force; but I've just come through a healing of my own past, something that had haunted me for years. So I think I know some of the signs."

'Hmm,' Peter mused silently. 'No one's ever called me Pops. I kinda like it.'

"Hmm," Peter mused aloud. "You think it was something I re-enacted from my past. That's intriguing." And Peter told Officer Aren his experience at the community. He talked and talked, and, in the midst of his sharing, a door opened to yet another wave of feelings. As he wept he began to remember the day the Emperor had nothing on at all. He remembered the townspeople egging him on to speak the truth aloud. He remembered his grownup friend, the baker, encouraging him to broadcast the truth throughout the village. He remembered them all making him the scapegoat. He remembered how everybody joined with the authorities to save themselves at Peter's expense.

Aren was right. It was another version of the same experience. He didn't want ever to go through this again. So he told Aren about the childhood version, hoping that would help him toward ending the pattern.

This ordinary cop was actually a very wise man. He talked to Peter about his experience with people and authority. "Until people develop a mature relationship with authority," he explained, "they have two ways of dealing with it. Both stem from their childhood experience with authority. One is to rebel against authority, openly or hidden. The other is to become one with authority, feeling that even if they don't like the authority, the oneness with it makes them safe."

"I see," Peter reflected. "So the people in the empire and the people in the community both enacted their rebellious side by egging me on.

And when the authority reacted, the people protected themselves by becoming one with the very authority they were rebelling against moments before."

"Ya've got it," replied Aren.

"How sad I got caught in the middle. How sad they didn't have the integrity to own up to their own rebellion."

"Yup!" said Aren. "That's true. But that's human nature, and ya need to be aware of that. It happens in religious and spiritual communities, military and police communities, and civilian communities all over the world. What's most important for ya, Pops, is to know that and to be conscious of yer own relationship with authority — outer authority, yer own inner authority, and the authority of the Divine Source."

"Hmm. Relationships with authority?" asked Peter.

"Yup. Ya need to tend to yer own relationship with authority. Ya need to make sure yerself is neither rebelling nor becoming one with authority in an unhealthy way. Ya need to develop the ability to stand firm with an authority who is in integrity, and to expose an authority who is misusing power. In other words, ya need to mature yerself so that ya can stand in the authority of yer Self, knowing clearly how yer using yer authority and how others are using theirs. Then ya'll not be a patsy to others egging ya on to act out their rebellion for them instead of doing their own work to mature their relationship with authority.

"Ya must already know, Pops, this work is challenging. It's the work of heroes and heroines. Ya'll never be able to mature yer relationship with authority without meeting the places in yer history where ya did not get what ya wanted from authorities, where ya did not get what ya needed from an authority, where some authority caused ya pain by misusing her authority, where some authority harmed ya by abusing his power as an authority. And ya cannot mature yer relationship with authority without meeting in yerself the parts that are tempted to misuse and abuse power and authority."

"Sounds true but painful. Right now, though, I can only focus on how you have helped me solve a mystery in a most mysterious way. What an extraordinary gift!"

"Mystery. Yes, Pops. Well, I am a policeman." Chuckling, Officer Aren put one hand on Peter's shoulder and extended the other in an invitation.

Peter reached out and grasped the officer's strong hand. "Thank you, friend. You have given me a taste of what I have been seeking."

HERE AND NOW

CHAPTER THIRTEEN
THERE'S ONLY ONE AUTHORITY HERE, AND I'M IT

Review . . .

The human dynamics in relation to authority can affect all our interactions. Our relationship with authority has its roots in childhood experiences with a mother, father, grandparent, aunt, uncle, sibling, teacher, and even God.

When Peter was a child, the villagers taunted him to speak out and then deserted him when the authorities reacted.

Peter grew up and thought he found a community where people could be close with each other and trust that everyone would be held sacred. But in a tension-filled exchange with others in the community, no one but Peter owned responsibility for the misunderstandings.

In great despair, Peter left the community. Officer Aren, an ordinary policeman, came like an angel out of the blue. He talked with Peter about his experience with people and authority. Peter discovered that he needed to become conscious of his own relationship with authority.

Consider . . .

We never know who will come to serve us in a way deeper than we ever consciously considered possible.

Officer Aren taught Peter about his relationship with authority. Look at your childhood experiences with authorities — mother, father, grandparents, aunts and uncles, older siblings, nanny, teacher, and even God.

❖ Of these authority figures, which had the greatest positive impact on your relationship with authority? Why? How?

❖ Which undermined your confidence in authorities? Elaborate on each.

Most likely you have been an authority figure in some way — as a parent, in a position of leadership in a social club, or being the driver of your carpool.

❖ When have you used the power inherent in your position well?

❖ Have you sometimes felt tempted to wield it inappropriately?

❖ Think of one instance where you misused your power.

❖ How might you prevent that from happening in the future?

And Then . . .

Peter left Officer Aren that day, grateful for the grace that had connected them. He went to his home to grieve the loss of the community as *home* . . . but he was on the way, someday when he was ready, to do the inner work about authority. This work would help him claim his inner Self as home.

HAUNTED BY HISTORY

Finally, a block away from the castle, a little child's voice was heard saying, "But the Emperor has nothing on at all!"

The child's mother said, "I command you to change your words! Say 'The Emperor may appear to have nothing on at all, but he is really dressed in fine garments woven of silk and gold threads.'"

"But, Mama," replied the child, "that is not true."

"If you want your dinner tonight, child, you will say what I tell you."

The child turned toward his father and said, "Daddy, the Emperor has nothing on at all."

His father answered, "Don't think that! Control your thoughts and words, child, or you will be in big trouble. Just tell the Emperor he looks wonderful, and believe it. Then everything will be fine. If you don't, then you can forget your bedtime story and goodnight hug."

"But, Papa," responded the child, "that is not true. Mama. Papa. That is not true. How can you do this? What you're doing isn't fair. It isn't right."

And at the same time the child's mother was saying, "No dinner!" his father said, "No story! No hug!"

The child's insides were all knotted up. He had difficulty breathing. And he stood there shaking, saying to himself, "I just can't win, no matter what I do."

Steven grew up. He no longer remembered the day the Emperor had nothing on at all. Although he was an intelligent man, he didn't act intelligent. He had trouble speaking. He had trouble thinking. He had trouble following through with anything important. He had come to a point in his life at which everything was at risk — his job, his marriage, his parenting, his friendships, and his volunteer work at the church. The minister who had been counseling Steven was at the limit of his abilities and feeling somewhat distraught himself. Finally he suggested Steven see the famous psychic healer, Miss Trudy. "I know you are not physically ill," offered Reverend White, "but perhaps Miss Trudy can help you out of this dilemma before your body does take it on."

Trusting his minister, Steven made an appointment with Miss Trudy. He found out he could tape the session so he could listen to it over and over again, and he was happy about that. He hoped it would help him relax and be in the moment with her.

Welcoming him into her office, Miss Trudy took a look at his physical body and his energy field. Then she popped the cassette he had brought into the tape recorder, pressed the record button, and before he had a chance to say anything or find out anything about her, began speaking: "Steven, you are living in a drugged condition. You might as well be asleep. Your past has overtaken you and has you in its spell. You are addicted. If you don't snap yourself out of it, you will likely die of an overdose of your own history.

"No more going back to the past to ruminate on old events. No more endless questions, especially those beginning with 'what if.' No more being careless with your words. Stop saying things like 'I'm sick of this,' 'I wish she were dead,' or 'I could kill her.' You are only ruining your own karma. Think and speak only happy thoughts.

"The simple remedy for this addiction, Steven, is this: You have to control what you think. You have to command yourself to change what you say and what you do. You have to refuse to be a victim. If you come out of any experience saying things like, 'I knew it! I knew there was no way out,' or 'See! I knew all along I was a loser,' or 'That proves it! I just can't win no matter what I do,' then you have misunderstood and misinterpreted the experience. This is a matter of life and death, Steven, yours. That is all. Thank you for coming."

Steven felt her coldness covered with a mask of kindness. He felt her disdain toward him, despite the guise of wisdom. So much of what she had said and how she had said it didn't feel right to him. But in addition, there was a layer of his response that he couldn't identify. When he focused on discerning that layer, he felt all knotted up inside.

Abruptly, she stood up, and he stood, too. He paid her a lot of hard-earned money for a 15-minute reading that left him feeling battered. He numbly took the tape cassette out of her hand and left. He felt awful. It was difficult to breathe. He was shaking. His insides were still in knots. Outside Miss Trudy's office, Steven stood, disoriented, on the street.

People passed by him and didn't even notice him. Finally a young woman in her 20's stopped and asked him, "Are you all right, sir?"

"Sir?" he repeated to himself. That jolted him back to reality. He was only 40; did that make him a "sir"?

He tried to speak, appreciating her caring. But he couldn't get the words out. Not certain what was happening with this man, the young woman didn't want to leave him alone. She suggested they go to sit on a bench in the park across the street. And Steven agreed; or rather, he simply allowed her to take him to the bench.

"What's your name?" she asked gently.

"Uhh, Steven," he whispered, still in a daze.

"Mine's Mita." She extended her hand, wanting to help him feel as connected as possible. "Hi, Steven."

"Hi, Mita," he answered, barely audible, not yet ready for touch.

"Do you want to talk about it?" Mita invited, resting her hands lightly in her lap.

"I don't know if I can," was all he could say. Then, "Who are you, anyway? How can I talk to a young woman I met on the street, someone I don't even know?"

"Good point," she said as she remembered she was still a stranger to this man, who seemed to have lost his bearings. "I'm an actress, living here, building my skill and art. I have a passion for my work. I love the part where I feel my character. I've been in therapy for a long time to help me work through my own feelings and my own history, so I can step into someone else's and be authentic. Because my parents are both spiritual counselors, this has been a way of life for me since I was little."

She paused a moment, taking in his softening. Then, "I saw you by the door. You were shaking, and I could feel your distress. I couldn't just leave you there."

"Thank you, Mita. You are a kind young woman. I think God must have sent you to me, especially 'cause you are so at home with spiritual and therapeutic work. Maybe you can help me."

"I'll try," she said and looked at him with the most understanding, compassionate eyes. This made it so much easier for him to continue. He told her the whole story — what was going on in his life, Reverend White's counseling, his referral to Miss Trudy, everything he could remember of what Miss Trudy had said, and his many different reactions. He showed her the tape, which he had remembered to take before walking out. Then he sighed and was silent.

Mita told Steven that she happened to have a tape player in her purse and offered to listen to the taped session with him. His instinct was to trust this godsend and so he agreed.

They listened together, and then Mita began, "Steven, there are two major things to look at here. First, what Miss Trudy taught you and how damaging it was. And second, your reaction. It feels more intense and charged than just a reaction to her. My guess is there's something in your past that has been evoked by this encounter. Let's start with what she said. Okay?"

"Mm-hmm."

"Oops! I started right in without connecting with you, just like Miss Trudy did. Thank goodness I caught myself. I want to take a moment and talk with you heart-to-heart. I was feeling sad, Steven, that Miss Trudy didn't even bother to connect with you, and instead analyzed and preached at you. Having begun to do the same thing and then having caught myself, I feel even more pained that she just kept going. Without the connection, the distorted things she said are even more damaging.

"Although there are seeds of truth in some of her statements, her contempt and her distortions contaminate everything. Her contempt is a sign that she has not done her own healing work. Her distortions reflect a lack of her personal work and serious misunderstanding. She makes clear that she considers your history worthless and lets you know that in a disparaging manner. She talks about not revisiting your past, Steven, as though that will solve your problems. Failure to work through what's unresolved from our past causes our history to consume us, consciously or unconsciously. We can be fully and consistently present in the current moment only after we have truly made peace with our past. To me, her vehement dismissal of the past reveals that she has not worked through her own past."

Mita paused and asked, "How are you doing with these ideas, Steven?"

"What you're saying is helping me to settle down inside, Mita. But I'd like to know I will be able to remember what you're telling me. Could we tape-record our conversation?"

"Absolutely. Let's use the other side of the tape," suggested Mita. "Then you can listen to both sides a few times and see what resonates for you. You will know what best serves you."

She turned the tape over, cued it up, and pressed 'record.'

"Now let's see," she continued. "Miss Trudy speaks about controlling what you think. We can control our thoughts in many ways. We can distract ourselves from what we are thinking, by turning on the radio and singing. We can will ourselves to think something else, for example, reciting a poem or practicing a lecture. We can make ourselves think something different, like naming what we pass as we walk to work. We can bury our feelings and the thoughts attached to them without really knowing what those feelings and thoughts are. We can even channel our unpleasant feelings into some activity that is more acceptable than paying attention to them. All this without any awareness that our feelings are living things, imbedded in our living bodies."

"That sounds dangerous, Mita. I don't want to control my thoughts that way. She told me to change my words, not to speak about the past, to talk only about happy thoughts."

"Changing your vocabulary means that you lose the gems your inner voice is trying to give you to solve the mystery. Instead of changing my words, Steven, I would rather listen carefully to what my spontaneous words are saying as clues for healing the underlying mystery."

"Yeah, Mita. I've got a real mystery to solve. I need every clue I can get."

"That's right, Steven. Seems to me that Miss Trudy's approach throws away many important clues. For example, she says that you are misunderstanding an experience if you feel like a victim when you emerge from it.

"It is Miss Trudy who is misunderstanding, Steven. She does not get that if you finish an experience saying, 'That proves it! I just can't win no matter what I do,' you have brought back a gem for your healing. It means you have reclaimed from your past an early decision — something you decided about your life years and years ago. You may still believe this decision is the truth about life. But someone who truly knows and can assist you in the healing process will know that this is a crucial moment. In this instant, you are ripe to be shown how you are co-creating in your life without awareness.

"If instead of trying to persuade you to control your words and thoughts on the surface, Miss Trudy knew the healing that existed on deeper levels, she would take such an opportunity to teach you. She might tell you, 'Steven, in that memory you just revisited, you experienced being unable to win, no matter what you did. If you had been an adult, or if you had an adult's help, you would have known that was a single instance in your life. Or you would have known that was a single context in your life, but not your whole life or the whole universe.'

"She would continue, 'But since you had no way to know that, you went from having that experience to believing that is how it would always be everywhere. And then, Steven, without even realizing it, you took the belief you formed and turned it into a decision — *That proves it! I just can't win, no matter what I do.* You didn't know when you created this decision that you would then re-create the same kind of situation again and again in your life, so you could prove to yourself *you can't win no matter what you do.* Until you realize just what your early decision was, how can you change it?'"

"My thought, Mita, is that it's gonna be hard enough to change the early decision even when I know exactly what it is. Without knowing, changing it would be impossible."

Mita nodded, "But Miss Trudy doesn't know this depth of healing and so couldn't teach you all of that. There are so many people in the healing professions who have no real knowledge of the human psyche and soul and have failed to do their own work. Yet they put themselves forward as experts able to help other people grow and heal. Often there are elements of truth in what they teach; but the elements may then be distorted and misused. These healers do great harm to people as a result."

"Wait, wait!" Steven interrupted. "That phrase *I just can't win, no matter what I do* feels so familiar. I was just taken back to a memory from my childhood! It's just as you said. Something in my past was evoked by her. And this is it!"

"That's great. Can you tell me about it?" Mita was excited that Steven was becoming more and more an active co-creator in his own healing.

And Steven related all about the day the Emperor had nothing on at all. Most important of all, he told Mita the early decision he made that day when he was a child: *I just can't win, no matter what I do.* "When Miss Trudy said that, they were just words to me. I had to go back into my unpleasant memories in order to really know this as my own decision."

They celebrated his awareness. Both of them were ecstatic that having found the early decision, Steven could now do the work to change it in his mind, in his heart, in his body, in his energy, and even in his soul.

HERE AND NOW

CHAPTER FOURTEEN
HAUNTED BY HISTORY

Review . . .

Many people in the healing professions lack knowledge of the human psyche and soul and have failed to do their own healing work.

When he was a child, Steven's parents told him to control his thoughts and words or he would be in trouble.

Steven grew up and came to a point in his life at which everything was in jeopardy. A famous psychic, Miss Trudy, looked at his physical body and his energy field and told him the simple remedy was to "control what you think." Steven, like many of us, made decisions that continually drove his life. Miss Trudy's advice blocked Steven's way to the path of real healing — the discovery of his early life decision.

Steven left the psychic reading feeling battered. On the street, he met Mita, a young actress, who helped Steven work through his past. "Failure to work through what's unresolved from our past," she told him, "causes our history to consume us."

Consider . . .

We need to understand that a statement such as Steven's "I just can't win, no matter what I do," is not merely a core belief. Rather, it is a decision he made that will drive his co-creation with life ever after.

It is a sacred act to discover our own early decisions and how, through them, we continually create a maze-like version of reality, in which we go 'round and 'round in a vicious cycle. This discovery is a doorway into healing.

Imagine the impact created by the early decisions of our healers in different arenas of life. Picture a therapist who decided as a little boy, "When I grow up, I'm gonna tell the whole world what you did." See in your mind's eye the effect of a spiritual teacher who decided as a little girl, "When I'm bigger than you are, I'll have all the answers and no one will be able to challenge me anymore." And now conceive of the consequences of a government official whose early decision was, "You have the power now, but someday I'll have all the power."

We each make our own early life decisions. We each create our own maze. The only way out of the maze is to go through it consciously, uncovering the early decisions, feeling the pain of their original cause and of their cyclical effect. This, over time, will help us free ourselves.

❖ As you have read Steven's story, have any of your early decisions come into consciousness? What are they? Take three and find their origins and their effects on your life.

And Then . . .

Steven's experience with Mita was inspirational and expansive. He learned conceptually about his early decision and experienced the memory. But as we almost always do when we expand, Steven contracted.

Each person contracts in different ways at different times. For example, sometimes people tighten their muscles; sometimes people become critical of self and others; and sometimes people start to enter old destructive patterns.

No one had taught him that contracting was the usual response. No one had taught him that the contraction would offer great clues for his healing. No one had taught him to ride the contraction until he expanded again.

As a result, Steven was caught in the vicious cycle of his old way of thinking and used the contraction to prove his early decision was right: "I just can't win, no matter what I do."

I'LL HELP YOU BE ABUSIVE BY PRETENDING YOU'RE NOT

*F*inally, a block away from the castle, a little child's voice was heard saying, "But the Emperor has nothing on at all!"

The father smacked her on the side of her head. "Be quiet! You'll wreck everything!"

The mother kneed her in the small of her back. "Hush up, you'll ruin everything!"

Having lived under the rule of an abusive Emperor themselves, they whisked their child off, re-enacting with her what had been done to them. Upon arriving home, they pushed her down on the stoop and terrorized her by recounting all the horrible things that could happen if she didn't keep quiet about the Emperor's guise. Papa could lose his job, and it would be her fault. Mama could lose her students, and the child would be to blame. They could lose their home all because of her. They could lose their food and clothing. They could be humiliated publicly. They could end up beggars on the street with not a soul willing to help them, and it would be her fault alone. They could die if she didn't keep silent. And it would be all her fault!

"Why are you being so mean to me?" she asked plaintively.

"To wake you up to reality!" they shouted in unison.

They so filled their little girl with dread that it seemed she would never again be able to give voice to the truth when she saw it, terrified of being attacked and blamed.

Celestial grew up. She no longer remembered the day the Emperor had nothing on at all.

She knew only that her family had journeyed across the sea from a northern country to the land of possibility, and the opportunities she now had in her life seemed limitless.

As a young adult she found herself drawn to the world of spiritual healing, which gave her a venue through which to recover her voice. She could speak without risk, because the source was the spirit world. It was amazing! Celestial began to climb the ladder of success in the healing circuit (Chapter Four). With each step up the ladder, she gained a little more of her voice, and her ambitions grew. Who knew how far she would go?

Eventually she became a national celebrity, speaking her own spiritual mind all across the nation. The more spontaneous and free she became to speak the truth as she saw it, the more she was filled with a secret dread. She didn't understand it. She didn't explore it. She didn't let it stop her. Celestial just kept going.

She became so famous, so wealthy, and so powerful that she started her own company and began to sponsor the kind of workshops she had previously attended as a guest healer. Out of her good heart and her desire to share, she harnessed her longing to help others go past their fears to their dreams, as she had done. She was making a mistake, though, and didn't even realize it! For her own sake and for the sake of her students, Celestial should have known it is not possible to go past our fears. As a healer, she should have understood that we have to go through our fears in order to truly free ourselves from them. Otherwise, our fears will create experiences in our lives without our knowledge or conscious consent.

Celestial mostly did her workshops solo. Every once in awhile she found a spiritual teacher she invited to join her as a guest. Most of the guests were action-oriented rather than feeling-oriented. Most of them worked at a level deeper than that of the audience, but still very close to the surface. These guests, without Celestial's even knowing it, colluded with her defense against her own secret feelings and with her audience members' defenses against their feelings. But of course, when people go to a body-mind-spirit workshop, they are not expecting to feel because the heart has been left out. And not many complain, for often when they are defending against feelings, they are glad to have people assist their cause.

In this way, even the very spiritual Celestial became vulnerable to people who were oversimplifying truth, to people who were teaching distortions of the truth, to people who were teaching seeds of truth twisted, hardened and packaged into lies. She became susceptible to people who delivered kernels of truth with contempt. She became seducible by people who were misusing their power under the guise of healing.

One day, Celestial met Ralph Young, a psychiatrist from the East. A mutual friend had introduced them, and he turned out to be a great help and comfort to Celestial as she rose to fame through her workshop tours. It wasn't long before she realized she had fallen in love with Ralph. He became aware of his feelings for her, too, and they became a team — both in their personal lives through marriage, and in their professional lives as authorities in the workshop circuit.

She still had the secret fear, but Celestial gave herself to living the wonderful life of which she had dreamed.

Celestial and Ralph traveled the world doing workshops together. He did the psychology part and she the spiritual aspect. Thousands and thousands of people tried to buy tickets for their events. They already knew of Celestial's popular and powerful workshops. Now they wanted to see the expert couple. They gave their trust to Ralph, too, because she transferred it by bringing him into her professional arena and into her marriage bed. If Celestial could trust him that much, of course they would, too.

After the couple had proven themselves on the workshop circuit, a famous producer from the national broadcasting system wanted to film one of their workshops and air it on television. The show was filmed in the fall and was widely advertised as the holiday showing approached.

As the show opened, Celestial and Ralph celebrated their success and discussed segments from the workshop.

At one point the following segment was shown:

> *A woman in the group, Rosemary, told Ralph of her dilemma with her husband. He had hurt her again and again, and now she didn't trust him.*
>
> *Ralph gently began with her, "You have been deeply hurt by your husband, haven't you? You've tried and tried, turned yourself inside out, and there has been no repair, has there? You want so much to resolve this with him, don't you?"*
>
> *Then he told her abruptly and harshly, "But the truth is, if you don't trust your husband, it's because you have trust issues. Maybe your parents hurt you, and you developed a defense of not trusting anybody. Maybe your parents undermined your trust in yourself when you saw things clearly and they denied them. I'd lay odds that you wouldn't know who is trustworthy and who isn't. I'll bet you don't trust me. But it's not about me. Everyone else here trusts me. It's about you and your trust issues."*

When the cameras returned from the taped gathering to Celestial and Ralph live, Celestial said, "My goodness, Ralph! In the workshop, I was uncomfortable with how you treated that woman, but I followed your lead and expanded the teaching with her. As I watch the clip, though, that seems cruel to me. It doesn't seem right that you were so cruel to her."

Ralph answered her, "Our job, Celestial, is to wake people up to reality, to bring them out of their drugged, sleepy state into reality. That's what I was doing. That's what I always do, you know that."

"I do know that, Ralph. And you've got me in reality now," Celestial replied with a twisted little smile.

Ralph continued, "What good is it going to do people to pay hundreds of dollars to us and have us let them stay in their crazy, hazy, drowsy existence?"

Halfway across the country a spiritual teacher named Mita watched Celestial name Ralph's cruelty and then submit to and enable it. It broke her heart to watch Celestial silently support and collude with Ralph while he abused not only his power — the power she had loaned him and helped him build — but also the people in the workshop and the millions of viewers who would see this across the world.

It distressed her to see that people were so accustomed to abuse they gobbled up Ralph's dictums and directions for achieving their goals without paying any attention to the abusiveness of the process. He and Celestial received hundreds of thousands of letters thanking them for what they were doing, which demonstrated how oblivious people were to his abusiveness. Imagine being abused and saying "thank you" for it! It showed how blinded Celestial was by her own unhealed wounds of abuse and threats of abuse that she stood by allowing and supporting her husband, instead of seeing what he was doing, speaking about it, and refusing to help him act out such destructiveness. And it revealed how much in denial she was that when the letters arrived — including a couple from Mita — naming the abuse with heartfelt concern, Celestial never bothered to answer the letters, but rather spoke of them with contempt at press interviews and on her workshop tours.

It had been painful enough for Mita to hear about and watch Celestial be part of Ralph's abuse when Celestial seemed unaware. But here Celestial was naming it. Here Celestial was asking Ralph, "Why are you so cruel?" And after asking him and hearing his bizarre justification, here Celestial was allowing it.

Mita wished she could do something to help Celestial. She had been able to help complete strangers in so many ways: Finding them on the beach, meeting them in a public restroom, going up to them on the street. She couldn't offer Celestial a complimentary session or workshop. She couldn't get invited as a guest on Celestial's tour, since the kind of work Mita did cannot be done in a one-time adrenaline-surge workshop. Mita could find no way to connect directly with this international celebrity healer.

Yet, she could bear inaction no longer. She had to do something to help Celestial and the millions of people all across the world who were affected by Celestial's workshops daily. And something to help Ralph, or at least to stop him. Face-to-face with her own sense of impotence, Mita decided to tell a story portraying the vision of the outcome she desired.

She found her tape recorder, sat with it in her rocking chair in front of the window overlooking the waterfall, turned it on, and began. She told the whole story up to this point, and then continued . . .

I was guided to contact Celestial's closest relative from childhood, her cousin, Skye. It was a bold move. And who knew what the consequences would be? But I could not sit by, not speaking my voice, not saying the truth. I could not do the same thing Celestial was doing with Ralph. So I wrote to Skye.

As grace would have it, Skye was deeply affected by the truth and the heart of my letter. She said "yes" to a meeting with me, and after a very rich afternoon together, she agreed to talk to Celestial. Finally, Skye arranged for the three of us to come together. As we gathered, Celestial's demeanor revealed her ambivalence: in one moment extending herself, in the next withholding; in one moment open, in the next suspicious; in one moment undefended, in the next energetically striking out.

I extended my hand and my heart to Celestial. "Thank you so much for meeting with me. It is a reflection of your good heart and positive intention that I have so often felt and known. It fills my own heart with hope."

Hesitating, Celestial replied with curt tone yet open visage, "You're welcome." Then after a deep sigh, she looked into my eyes and said, "Thank you so much for knowing who I really am in my heart and intention."

With a smile from deep within, I nodded. Then I turned to Skye and thanked her for making this connection. Skye reached out to Celestial and began, "My dearest cousin, Mita has helped open my eyes. We have been blind to what is 'off' in your partner, Ralph. Under the guise of healing, really he is abusive. I am so sorry that I have not been able to help you see this before.

"But now we are both awakening — with the gentle, loving help of Mita, here. And you, Celestial, were even beginning to see this for yourself. After all, you told Ralph on international television that he was cruel!"

A succession of conflicting expressions flitted across Celestial's face, reflecting her inner process. She reconsidered the question of Ralph's "cruelty" and then said, "Yes, I guess maybe I was right to call him cruel. Maybe he really is abusive." After a pause allowing the pieces to fall into place, she searched for answers aloud. "But what took me so long? Why couldn't I see before? Why couldn't I stop him? What damage have I done to my following? And what do I need to do?"

"Let's take one question at a time, Celestial," I answered, "and with care for your heart as we go."

"That is so different from what I've been experiencing with Ralph," cried Celestial, as waves of tears flowed from the ocean of her being.

"Yes, Celestial," I confirmed. "Feel that difference."

Skye and I sat in silence for a long time, witnessing and receiving Celestial's pain and sorrow. When the tide of her feeling went out, Celestial joined us in silence, then suddenly laughed, "I can feel! I can feel! I can feel things I wasn't able to feel before."

"Yes," I agreed. "We can feel when we experience that we are safe within ourselves and in the world outside us."

"But what took me so long?" Celestial asked again. "Why couldn't I see and feel before? And why couldn't I stop him?"

"Maybe you didn't feel safe enough, Celestial," I suggested. "Safe enough to see, safe enough to know, safe enough to let down your *defenses, safe enough to remember whatever this reminds you of from your past, safe enough to feel, and safe enough to act. Plus, remember, your relationship with Ralph is not just a working partnership but also your marriage partnership. Maybe you haven't felt safe enough at home to confront him with the ways in which he is not safe."*

"Yes," added Skye. "And it seems to me that this is a case of the 'Emperor's New Clothes.' Mita is like the innocent child who sees the truth, and we, Celestial, have been the adults, blinded by fear."

"Oh, my God!" replied Celestial. "Skye, you've hit the nail on the head. Ouch! Even I heard the violence in my metaphor." And Celestial began to share with Skye and me her experience of the Emperor and his new clothes, beginning with, "But I was the child! I was the child who saw and spoke; and I was the child who shrank away in terror." She paused, gulping hard.

"That's who I've been with Ralph, the child who shrank away in terror. And all along I thought I was a powerful benefactor and partner. Ugh! Not only has Ralph been the Emperor with no clothes on, pretending he was finely dressed, but so also have I been the Emperor without clothes, while appearing not to be."

"Please, Celestial, hold yourself with love as you walk through this," I urged, seeing that there was little for me to do at this point, save be there fully with Celestial, who seemed to be putting together the puzzle pieces just fine.

"I was terrified of seeing and saying what I saw," continued Celestial, "lest I be smacked on the side of my head, kneed in the small of my back, caused to lose everything, even my life, humiliated publicly. Oh, my God! What harm have I done to my thousands and thousands of workshop participants all over the world?"

"There are a few pieces that I see," I offered gently. Celestial accepted gratefully, and I said tenderly, "You have taught people that the ends do justify the means. You have taught them lies — that abuse and misuse of power are okay, and can, in fact, create healing. For your fans you

have modeled treating people with contempt and disdain; you have also modeled for them silence and submission in the face of abuse.

"You have demonstrated to them the avoidance of feelings, especially terror; you have shown them, by your example, that when we avoid our own terror, we invite into our lives the energy of the terrorizer. That energy may be in the form of another person whose terrorizing calls forth our buried terror to be felt and expressed. Or that energy may be in the form of a part of ourselves, an aspect within that terrorizes us or those around us. You have treated your viewers the way you were treated. You have helped others treat your viewers the way you were treated. Out of your unconsciousness, out of your own unhealed wounds, all this has happened."

Celestial gasped repeatedly as I told her these bitter truths. "I have to apologize. I have to find a way to set this right."

"Yes," I nodded, tears in my eyes, moved that she could so quickly and accurately take in all of this. Even as I looked at Celestial with tenderness and compassion, my heart celebrated the unveiling of the truth.

We broke for a walk in the morning sunlight, Celestial asking me to stay so we might plan together how to make a repair. I accepted with delight. To have my offer of help be so well received and have such a positive outcome was truly a blessing and a pleasure.

Mita paused. She leaned forward, turned off the recorder, stood and stretched. 'Time for a hot cup of tea,' she thought. Ten minutes later, she returned to her chair with a steaming mug, pressed 'record' once more, and resumed speaking.

We came back together after our walk and some time alone. Sitting in a circle, all three of us began to explore what Celestial needed to do and how to do it. I encouraged Celestial to find the answers in her heart. She began to weep.

"I'm afraid," she acknowledged between the waves of tears.

"I know," I soothed. "It's okay. Just let yourself feel the fear."

And Celestial did. She trembled with fear. She shook with fear. She curled into a ball with fear. She shrieked with fear. Skye and I stayed with her, allowing her fear to touch the vestiges of our own. And nobody tried to force anyone out of their fear, for by that time, we all knew that the only way out of one's fear is to go all the way through it. Not to force oneself through it, but simply to feel the unfolding movement of the fear and allow it to release.

Celestial couldn't help but notice and comment on how different this was from the way Ralph managed and pushed people through their fear, herself included; how he justified bullying and humiliating people to get them moving. And this realization called forth more fear and also horror at the abuse with which she was complicit. Horror that having not felt her own terror, she had helped to inflict upon others terror of an international scale.

Skye and I were patient, tender, loving attendants who knew how to wed these qualities with truth. Not simply our subjective truth, but the undefended, innocent truth of the child who knew the Emperor had nothing on at all. We spent the afternoon helping Celestial birth her long-buried feelings. I knew that if Celestial could stay in this birthing process, her feelings themselves would become midwives to answers that would serve everyone.

As dusk came, Celestial sat in silence at last. For a long time, none of us spoke. All that was audible within our circle was the breath of life, which is Spirit. When Celestial spoke at last, her voice and her energy were changed. There was a new depth and clarity, a long-awaited fullness and authenticity to her presence.

"I need to talk to Ralph," Celestial began. "I need to tell him what I've realized. I will apologize to him for my blindness, my complicity, for not stopping him. I will encourage him to get help for his destructiveness. If it is all right with you, Mita, I will recommend he speak to you."

I nodded.

"I will tell him I am going to do another public broadcasting show, a special, so that I may apologize to everyone and begin to repair the harm I've done. I will cancel Ralph's part in my workshops, save perhaps one in which he apologizes himself, if he chooses." She shuddered and shook her head, "He's not going to like this."

"Perhaps not," I agreed. "But while one aspect of him may not like it, another will be so grateful that you are stopping him. It must be terrifying to him on a very deep level to have been allowed to do so much harm without anyone standing big enough to say 'no.' It's along the same lines as a two-year-old having temper tantrums in the midst of adults who are afraid and therefore unable to protect him and themselves. Such children are truly terrified, even though at the same time they look and act like happy tyrants."

"Hmm! I see what you mean," answered Celestial. "I will talk to Ralph, even if he doesn't like it. I will do what I need to. After all, I am not a little girl any more. He is not my father about to smack me on the side of my head. He is not my mother about to knee me in my back. And he is not the Emperor with the power to destroy me and my life. You are right, Skye. He is very much like the Emperor who has nothing on at all. And this very well may affect our marriage, too.

"Nevertheless, as I did when I was such a little girl, once again, I have to say the truth in public. The truth about him. And the truth about me."

Mita again shut off the tape recorder. She took her mug to the sink and began rinsing it. As she did, Mita wondered how Celestial would do her own cleanup. A few minutes later, returning to her rocker, she continued recording.

Celestial scheduled and paid for three airings of the repair program: One in a daytime slot, one during evening prime time, and one in a late-night slot. While there was no live audience, she was committed to giving everyone a chance to experience this program.

She made the setting for the show sacred, not to distract from her truth-telling, but rather to help hold it, to help hold her, to help each viewer to hold it all. She had a simple circular coffee table beside her, covered with a piece of black cloth. Upon it was a round, pure white, three-wicked candle, lighted. And Celestial sat on a round stool, the same height as the table. Skye and I, unseen by the viewing audience, were in the wings, each on one side of the stage.

The cameras were turned on. Celestial said a prayer aloud. "Dear God. I have, without even realizing it, made grave mistakes. Mistakes that have caused harm to people all over the world. Harm that people may experience consciously. But also harm that may have had its impact beneath consciousness, to work its effects unknown to people. I ache to set things right. I burn inside to make repair. I commit to helping people recover from what I have done.

"I do not know how this will unfold. I only know where I must begin: Speaking the truth about what I have done, about what has happened as a consequence. Please, God, be with me. Guide me. Hold me. Help me every step of the way. And please, God, help the people I have hurt. Protect us all."

Celestial sat in silence for a moment and then began speaking to the viewers. She began with the story of the Emperor who had nothing on at all. Celestial risked self-revealing, and she shared her story. She explained that the terror she felt that day was unbearable — to that little girl. But that unhealed, it seemed like it was also unbearable to her grown self. She acknowledged that although she spoke out about lots of things, secretly she still suffered from fear that prevented her from seeing and speaking the truth about many other things.

With tears streaming down her cheeks, Celestial continued, "Out of my own blind and unhealed state, I have brought you an imperfect teacher. Of course, we are all imperfect. But I have brought you a teacher who is capable of dealing with only a small piece of the whole. As a result, you have been taught distortions and half-truths, illusions and even lies wrapped in appealing cover by a man who seemed very sure of himself and was terribly convincing. He had me fooled. I am so very sorry." Looking straight at the camera, she allowed tears to flood her face.

Celestial continued. *"I taught you and modeled for you to avoid feelings. The very feelings we need to be alive, to heal, to become ourselves, to connect. I taught you it was okay to function, to do good things, to achieve, but not to feel. Especially not to feel fear. I taught you it was barely okay to cry if something was deeply moving. I taught you it was not okay to let go and weep if something was painful. But most of all, I did not want to feel my fear; so I taught you not to feel yours. And when teaching you 'to function your feelings away' didn't work, I used contempt to chase them away. And when that didn't work, I used teachings of the Divine to get you to spiritualize away your feelings. Oh, my God! I am so, so sorry."*

Celestial wept openly and deeply. When the wave of feeling was over she began again.

"We are in a time in our world when we are determined to end terrorism. We cannot spend all of our energy stopping terrorism only in the outer world. We must also end terrorism in our inner worlds. I must feel the terror I felt when I was terrorized by my parents. I must go all the way through that terror to the healing. And I must dissolve the currents in me that defended against that terror by terrorizing myself and others.

"Out of my denial, my unconsciousness, and my defenses against feeling my own terror, I have been complicit in terrorizing you — each time you participated in one of my workshops with Ralph. Because I had blocked my terror, I could not feel how frightened I became when he was cruel. I could not feel how frightening he was when he was cruel. I could not feel your pain and fear when he bullied and humiliated a volunteer from the group. I dared not feel the fear when he was abusive, lest I be catapulted back into my childhood memories of being terrorized. I was just glad I was his wife and friend and hoped that would protect me.

"Mostly I didn't even notice. A very few times, I tried to smooth things out with the workshop participants. Once in a while I made a joke about his brutality. Once I even asked him why he was so cruel and then okayed his absurd justification.

"Through Ralph, I taught you that the ends do justify the means — which is not true! Through Ralph, I taught you that misuse and abuse of power are acceptable, welcome, even entertaining — which is a lie! Through Ralph, I taught you that healing can come through abuse — which is ridiculous! I allowed him to treat you the way I was treated as a child. In this way, although unconsciously, I became a silent partner in the abuse. Even though I was not mean to you, cruel to you, bullying and humiliating, I stood by and allowed that to happen in my workshop."

Celestial bent her head and sobbed. She moved to her knees beside the altar she had created. The studio was silent except for her sobbing. Then Celestial blew her nose, wiped her face, and began speaking again.

"It is my intention and my heart's desire to make right what I have done. I don't know yet quite how to do that. I welcome your letters and e-mails. I will respond to them in some way, whether individually or in my workshops. In any way that is truth for both of us, I will make every effort to help you heal the wounds I have helped to cause — even if they were a re-enactment of something you had already experienced in your life.

"As for myself, I am going to work with a spiritual teacher, who has also been a therapist, to heal my wounds so that I don't perpetuate them with you. I am going to cancel my workshops with Ralph. I have already spoken with him and encouraged him to do his own healing work with someone who is qualified to help him go to the roots. He will have to decide for himself if he will apologize to you.

"That is all I know at this point. I will pray to be guided. I will pray to co-create with God and with you a deep, full, and fair repair. I don't expect immediate forgiveness. I hope, when the time is right, that *you will forgive me. I give thanks to those who helped bring me to this awareness: God. My sweet cousin, Skye. And Mita, a spiritual teacher, who kept reaching out to me until I finally listened and believed her. I am so grateful."*

Celestial looked straight into the camera, making eye contact and heart contact with every person who was watching. "And I am grateful for each of you." Then she bowed her head. The lights went out. And only the flames of the three-wicked candle remained.

A smile on her face, Mita turned off the recorder, closed her eyes, and rocked herself to sleep. When she awoke, she made a copy of the tape and put it on her altar. She placed the original carefully in a velvet pouch with a note saying, "Dear Celestial, This is my vision. With hope and prayers, Mita."

She inserted the pouch into a padded envelope, addressed the envelope, walked to the Federal Express office, and shipped her vision to Celestial. She walked home with a spring in her step, knowing that even if Celestial never listened to the tape, she, Mita, had already made an offering to Spirit that was healing for the whole world.

HERE AND NOW

CHAPTER FIFTEEN
I'LL HELP YOU BE ABUSIVE BY PRETENDING YOU'RE NOT

Review . . .

Workshop leaders, authors on book tours, and celebrity television and radio talk show hosts, often untrained or compelled to supply a quick fix, can model abusive behavior. Yet, their followers seem so accustomed to abuse that they gobble up their dictums and directions without noticing the abusiveness of the process.

When she was a child, Celestial's parents hushed her, so she would not "ruin everything," filling her with dread of giving voice to the truth.

As an adult, Celestial became a national celebrity on the workshop circuit, speaking her spiritual mind all across the nation (Chapter Four). Her personal and professional partner was Ralph Young, a psychiatrist. Out of fear of giving voice to the truth, Celestial colluded with his abusive leadership, causing harm to the audience participants seeking their help. This also spread harm to any people present who might model their behavior after Celestial and Ralph's behavior.

Having witnessed the public workshop with Rosemary, a spiritual teacher named Mita imagined a meeting with Celestial, which would open the famous spiritual healer to soul-searching. Celestial would realize she must go through her fears and face them or they would hold her captive for the rest of her life. Then she would apologize to her millions of fans and begin to repair the damage she had wrought.

Consider . . .

If we told the truth and were punished, if we wanted the truth and heard lies, if it was dangerous to be in truth, if it was frightening to know the truth, then we were wounded by such experiences. Because of these wounds, we may find ourselves deaf, dumb, blind, and paralyzed in the face of the crucial need to know the truth and respond to it.

Many people in our world today feel a threat deep in their cells in relation to speaking truth. The fears often go way beyond what might happen in their own life — as though it came from another lifetime or from what the human race holds in its collective consciousness. Some people, convinced that telling the truth will bring them only ill, worry they will be left penniless and homeless if they do speak truth. Some fear they will be shunned, outcast, exiled. Others live in dread that they will be hunted down, attacked, tortured, burned at the stake, crucified. In each of these cases, the root problem is some version of the early decision: "If I tell the truth, I will be destroyed."

Those who have no awareness of the early decision focus instead on the consequences they most fear.

❖ Do you sometimes feel endangered when you are about to speak the truth?

❖ Are you afraid what you say will not be accepted?

❖ Are you afraid you will not be accepted for saying it?

❖ Do you fear the consequences will be greater than you can even imagine?

Such feelings are clues to childhood experiences that have wounded your relationship to truth. Take a few moments right now and see if an awareness of the childhood roots comes into your consciousness.

And Then . . .

Celestial received Mita's tape in the velvet pouch. Touched to the core by Mita's vision, she made arrangements to visit Mita and hear more. The two spent hours together, each receiving great gifts from the exchange: Mita, the gift of having an impact that would affect millions of people the world over; Celestial, the gift of Mita's clear mirroring and heartfelt wisdom. As they closed their time together, Celestial promised, "I can't say I'll carry out the repair exactly as you have visioned it, Mita, but I do commit to a repair that will affect people as broadly as possible."

YOU MUST DO THIS FOREVER TO BE LOVED

Finally, a block away from the castle, a little child's voice was heard saying, "But the Emperor has nothing on at all!"

The child's mother nudged him. The child's father shook his finger at him. The little child said, "What? What? The Emperor has nothing on at all!"

The child's father looked down at him and said, "We're trying to do something here. If you ruin it, I'll have your head."

The child bent his head in shame and fear. His mother stooped down to meet him eye to eye. She said, "Sometimes we have to use what's occurring to get what we want. If you don't be quiet, you will spoil what we are trying to make happen. You don't want to do that, do you?"

The child tearfully shook his head.

"So be a good little boy, hold my hand, and be as quiet as a mouse," finished the mother.

The child reached for her hand, and they walked together down the road, following the Emperor in his procession. Several blocks away they reached the gate in the great walls surrounding the empire. Approaching the gate was a King from a neighboring land, coming for a state visit. He rode his horse in through the gate, and upon seeing the Emperor parading in nothing but his underwear, began to laugh without control.

While the people in the crowd kept up their pretense, the mother whispered to the father, "He is so humiliated he will have to change his ways now."

The child couldn't bear what was happening. He could hear snickers all around him, even though the people were trying to be serious. He didn't know what the Emperor had done that upset his mother and father so, but he felt sorry for the old man. He ran to the tailor's shop and asked if he could borrow a cape for a friend. The tailor readily loaned him a black velvet wrap.

The little boy ran to the gate and offered the cape to the Emperor, who, red with shame, fell to his knees and reached, not for the garment, but rather for the little boy. Walking around the sobbing Emperor, the little boy draped him in the velvet cape, then stood before him.

"Thank you, my child," said the Emperor, his arms wrapping around the child's little body. "I love you. You have saved me where no one else could. In your innocence and purity, you have pulled me out of a life of lies and abuse of the sacred power of my position. How can I ever repay you?"

"Well, I didn't understand most of what you said, but I do know you don't have to repay me, sir. You just have to tell all the people you're sorry and find the help to fix it so it never happens again."

"But you have already helped me," replied the Emperor.

"No, sir. I have only helped you to wake up. Now you need one of your royal counselors to help you do the work."

"All right . . . " he said hesitating, "but will you come visit me and talk with me?"

"Of course," said the child. "And will you come visit with me and talk with me?"

"As long as I live," pledged the Emperor.

The townspeople cheered and cheered. "The boy has saved our Emperor! The boy has saved our town!"

The visiting King and his troops cheered and cheered. "A boy has saved an empire. A boy has saved an empire. May we have such a boy in our kingdom if we ever need one."

And person after person passed by the child, thanking him for what he had done.

Merle grew up. He no longer remembered the day the Emperor had nothing on at all.

He was a student of pastoral counseling at a seminary in a large midwestern city. The director, Owen, was internationally acclaimed for his knowledge, his intuition, and his success with clients. Merle was delighted to be working with him and excited about how much he was learning.

But there were times when Merle was very uncomfortable with the teacher's arrogance about his wisdom and expertise. And it seemed that on some occasions Owen was thrilled with Merle's abilities, while on others Owen felt threatened. Merle didn't want to stifle himself; neither did he want to rub Owen's nose in his growing talent. What a challenge!

During one special training weekend, the seminary was holding practice oral exams to help students prepare to take their final examinations. Merle attended in order to learn what the process would be like, even though he was not anywhere near ready to take the exams. What he observed shocked him.

Of course, he had experienced Owen's imperious attitude before. One incident that stood out in his memory was when he had gone to talk to Owen about the possibility of opening his own pastoral counseling center. Owen's verbal response: "You may be a pastoral counselor, Merle, but unlike me, you don't have the leadership skills to run a whole center." His underlying response: I'll always be superior to you, Merle.

During the mock orals, Owen was behaving publicly as Merle had seen him act only in private before. His mask of charm was slipping. His veil of mature leadership was shredding. In place of teaching and preparing, Owen was acting like an adolescent bully, taking his revenge on someone from his past by "getting" his students. Merle could see signs of the bully in the smirk at the corner of Owen's mouth.

He asked trick questions. He posed questions to which there were many answers, but he would settle only for *his* answer. He picked to serve as mock examiners students who had never been through the exam process. And with snide remarks, he prodded them to make it difficult for the examinees. He even modeled for several newcomers how to toy with the person being tested. And when an exam was over and the student had barely made it through the gauntlet, Owen made fun of him while pretending to teach him how to correct his weaknesses.

Merle was sickened by what he was witnessing, yet no one else seemed to notice. To his dismay, he did not hear or see a hint of awareness in any of his fellow students. Because he felt so alone, he wondered if it were possible that others in the training group did notice but were afraid to confront the professor. He hoped if that were true, they would somehow let themselves be known.

Merle sat through the day, focused on staying present and constantly searching for what to do. He wanted to shout. He felt the impulse to run. He experienced the urge to shake Owen. He had moments of wishing he had never come to this seminary. Finally the afternoon session was over and the group prepared to go to dinner together. A couple of classmates asked Merle if he was all right. He thanked them for their concern and said he was working with some difficult things in his heart.

As everyone began walking to the restaurant, Merle stayed with his group but walked at the rear to give himself some space to process what was taking place. Being city-savvy, when he heard someone running up behind him, he turned around to assess his safety. It was Owen, who then slowed his pace to match Merle's.

They started talking. Rather, Owen started talking to Merle, bragging about the day and what he'd done for his students. Owen mistook Merle's silence for rapt attention and admiration. And that mistake led to another. Owen began speaking about Craig, the last student of the day to take a mock exam. It was disturbing to Merle to hear Owen assess another student. Owen actually gloated to Merle, "I'm gonna really crucify Craig tomorrow when he does his second mock oral."

Owen had just handed him something tangible enough to act on. He cared for his classmate and was not going to let Craig be abused. He was not going to leave Owen in a position where, left to his own devices, he would cause harm. He knew he must confront his teacher.

"Owen," Merle began, "what you are doing is dangerous. I can't collude with you by staying silent. I can't let you do it. If I see you trying to 'crucify Craig' tomorrow, I will right then tell the whole training group what you said tonight."

Owen was silent for three long blocks. Merle didn't know how his teacher would answer him. He expected Owen to say, "I'm trying to do something here. If you ruin it, I'll have your head." Or perhaps Owen would say, "Sometimes we have to use what's occurring to get what we want. If you don't be quiet, you will spoil what I am trying to accomplish. You don't want to do that, do you?"

Waiting in dread for Owen to talk to him, Merle found himself in a journey through time and space. He traveled back to a place where he spoke the truth about a leader — the Emperor who had nothing on at all — and his parents silenced him so their plan to force the leader to change could be carried out. Whew, no wonder this experience was so very intense! No wonder speaking out to Owen had such a profound impact on his own mind, heart, body, and soul.

Owen's voice brought Merle out of his depths and back to the city streets. Owen blustered and deflected. "You took me seriously, Merle? Don't be silly. Do you really think I would do that? I was only joking."

Merle stood his ground, "Yes, Owen. You were serious. What you were thinking and speaking is dangerous. I won't be silent about it."

Owen was quiet. Then haltingly he began, "Oh . . . my . . . You're right, Merle. Dear God! What I almost did! Thank you so much, Merle. You have stopped me from doing something cruel to Craig and damaging to the training group. You are such a brave and honest young man. I am so grateful. How can I repay you?"

"You don't have to repay me, Owen," replied Merle. "You simply need to apologize to Craig, to the training group as a whole, and get the help to heal this within yourself so that it doesn't happen again."

"I will. I will," agreed Owen. "But would you do the work with me? You're the only one who sees it. Will you help me, Merle? Please?"

"Owen, maybe I'm one of many who see it. There may be others who are afraid to say anything to you. And I'm the only one you spoke to saying, 'I'm gonna crucify Craig tomorrow . . .' By doing that you gave me an opening. And, no, Owen, I can't work with you. I'm the student here. You're the teacher. It's not my job to take care of you. Although, believe me, I am deeply honored that you would ask. But I still have so much to learn from you, including how a wound this serious can be healed and transformed."

"I understand," Owen came back again, "but will you at least tell me if you see me doing the same kinds of things in the future?"

"I will, Owen," answered Merle, "but I'd rather you not put the responsibility on me. It's really not my task. At the same time, you can be assured I will not go blind at this point of the journey."

"Good, Merle," replied Owen. "Thank you again. I love you. In your own way, you are a savior. You protected everyone. You even kept me from being publicly humiliated. What a kind person you are!"

Now standing in front of the restaurant, Owen reached out to hug Merle. With arms around his student, he began to sob. Loving yet awkward, Merle stood embracing his teacher. It was nice to be appreciated for what he had done. It was sweet to be loved for his courageous act.

But something still didn't feel right. Although he didn't know what, he committed himself to finding out.

That night, Merle had a dream. In the dream there were two storytellers. One, Aren, was telling him the story of what had happened in his life — both with the Emperor and with Owen.

When Aren finished the tale, the other storyteller, Mita, turned to Merle and asked, "What's missing, Merle? What doesn't feel right?"

Merle gave her question careful thought and then answered, "I don't know."

Mita answered her own question. "Neither the Emperor nor Owen simply expressed appreciation to you, although the essence of what they were actually saying was 'thank you.' Instead, they both claimed love for you, which was not really love at all. They merely *claimed* love for you because you saved them, not because you are Merle. That's why you feel so empty. In the world of these two men, if you honestly believe they love you, you are missing what really happened. And if you honestly believe they love you, in order to be loved, you will have to keep saving them."

HERE AND NOW

CHAPTER SIXTEEN
YOU MUST DO THIS FOREVER TO BE LOVED

Review . . .

People longing for love or to have an impact can be seduced by praise for what they have done, unaware they are missing out on recognition for who they are.

When he was a child, Merle's parents silenced him because they had a plan to force the Emperor to change his ways. But when the King from a neighboring land came for a state visit, the child draped the naked Emperor in a black velvet wrap. The Emperor thanked the child, declaring, "I love you. You have pulled me out of a life of lies and abuse of the power of my position."

Merle grew up and was a student of pastoral counseling at a seminary. The internationally acclaimed director, Owen, thanked Merle for preventing him from abusing his power, "Thank you. I love you. In your own way, you are a savior." Merle mistook his appreciation for real caring and affection.

Two storytellers in a dream told Merle of the pattern in his life both with the Emperor and with Owen: "In the world of these two men, if you honestly believe they love you, then you will have to keep saving them in order to be loved." This insight began Merle's healing.

Consider . . .

"The Emperor's New Clothes," retold in Chapter Two, ends without resolving the misuse of power. Although the child speaks the truth, the Emperor doesn't alter his course of action.

Chapter Sixteen offers a new ending. It may appear to be the perfect ending, but be careful as you discern the truth. The child has an impact on the Emperor and is thanked and congratulated by everybody. Many people, longing to have an impact, would welcome such a response. Don't be fooled! The people's praise for the child is based on what he has done for the Emperor and the town. The child himself and who he is are neither seen nor celebrated.

This seemingly ideal but ultimately unsatisfying ending is repeated in the true-to-life story. Owen doesn't merely thank Merle. He claims to love him. Again, don't be misled!

Owen does not really love *Merle*. He loves that Merle has met his needs. He loves that he has been rescued. His feeling is not really about Merle but rather about *himself*.

If Merle doesn't see the truth of this, he will be compelled to keep on doing what he has done in order to feel appreciated and loved. Yet if he buys the guise, he will never feel appreciated and loved simply for who he is.

Have you had the experience of being loved simply for who you are? Remember and describe it.

And Then . . .

Owen did apologize to the training group and to Craig, as he had promised. He also found a fine therapist at his own level of experience and began his healing process in earnest. Merle continued in the training group — to be a presence to hold Owen accountable for fulfilling the repair to which he committed, to experience that repair, and to serve his own learning and healing.

TOWARD HAPPILY
EVER AFTER . . .

FORGIVENESS: THE REAL THING

F inally, a block away from the castle, a little child's voice was heard saying, "But the Emperor has nothing on at all!"

When the Emperor smacked his daughter for her impudence, the child bit his hand in an involuntary act of self-protection. The Emperor was astounded and enraged. "I will never forgive you," he shouted to his only child and then sent her into exile.

His daughter was thunderstruck. She was scared and hurt to be smacked and yelled at by her father. She was crushed to be sent away from him, for she loved him so.

Time passed, and he did not send for her. She felt helpless and despairing. Still, she wrote home periodically, asking his forgiveness. But his heart had turned stone cold on that day he had nothing on at all.

Beth grew up. She never forgot the day her father, the Governor, had banished her to a boarding school in a different state. She lived her life in exile — praying that someday her father would forgive her, bringing her out of isolation and into reunion with him, her mother, her family, her people, and her home. But alas! She waited and waited to no avail.

Meanwhile, her father, John, governed his state with the guise of down-home patriarch covering an ever-growing rigidity, hard-heartedness, and cruelty. All of his constituents knew this came from the day he had exiled his daughter. And John never forgot, not for a moment, that horrible day his little girl had publicly exposed and humiliated him.

Years passed. John began having nightmares. Always the same theme — that day he cut off his daughter. But the variations were terrifying and mystifying to him. One dream was a realistic memory of the event. The next was simply darkness. Another dream was a caricature of him furious at her. There was the dream portraying him as a crazed wild animal. Still another revealed him as a raging baby.

Tormented by his dreams, John was afraid to sleep. He became exhausted. Finally unable to carry out his daily tasks, he asked his personal assistant to find him a therapist skilled in dream interpretation. One after another, he consulted each therapist on the list his assistant had prepared for him. All offered their advice, but without success. The dreams continued.

Weeks later, finally at the last name on the list, John called Aren. He seemed to John different from the others. Appearances did not matter to this man. He was simple and grounded, easily made a genuine connection with John, seemed very wise, and radiated hope.

Aren sat with John and listened for hours as the leader related his life story. Aren's empathy moved John in a way nothing ever had. The bond and trust that emerged created an unexpected openness in the hard-hearted Governor. As a result, when Aren spoke, John really listened.

"Some," Aren began, "might tell you these nightmares come from your not forgiving your daughter. Others might assert that it's not the absence of forgiving her but rather your swearing you will never forgive her. The second is a little closer than the first, for an intention to never forgive is very powerful, as are its consequences. But all these people who have come to help you have been focusing on an *act* of forgiveness. They have invited and urged, exhorted and pushed you toward telling your daughter you have forgiven her.

"No one has addressed what you need to go through to get to that act, if, in fact, it is a right act for you," Aren continued. "They have left the process out. Yes, you need to be willing to forgive her. Yes, you need to have an intention to go through the process. But, John, *this* process is not about your daughter, Beth. It is about you."

"What do you mean?" asked John.

"Forgiveness is not something you decide in your mind, John. You don't just think one day, 'I forgive this person,' and then it is done. It is a co-creation between a human being and Spirit. The person does the thorough inner work. Spirit gives the grace and the magic.

"Until this journey has been taken, it is premature to forgive. Without the fullness of these two aspects, real forgiveness is not possible."

"What about all the religious and spiritual teachings that tell us forgiveness is simply a choice?" John inquired.

"Many do teach immediate forgiveness," Aren acknowledged. "They impose an ideal upon the seeker. An ideal that cannot be achieved, only imitated or pretended through the mind and the behavior. These teachings interfere with the real emerging process of forgiveness in the heart, cells, and soul.

"Forgiveness, when it comes, John, is organic, not mimicked. It doesn't necessarily mean reuniting with the person forgiven, who may not be alive, accessible, or safe to interact with. She may have Alzheimer's disease. He may still be abusive. In these cases, the forgiveness needs to be from afar. And the focus is not on the broken relationship, but rather on the real hope of living future relationships in a way that will be more loving and trustworthy."

"What if the person is still alive?" John asked. "Both Beth and I are still alive."

Aren was quiet for a moment before he spoke. "If the one who has caused harm can hold himself accountable, can repair the breach, can make restitution, and can abstain from repeating the damage, then not only can the future of trust and love in other relationships be salvaged, but also the trust and love between the two parties can be restored. It takes time, though," Aren said calmly and with certainty. "It takes time, a process of healing, and trust."

"I don't know if I trust even the possibility," ventured John honestly.

"Perhaps until real forgiveness unfolds organically," returned Aren, "it must suffice to simply ask Spirit, as Jesus asked God, 'Please forgive this person, who does not know what he does.'"

"But what if the person does know?" protested John.

"That is important to discern, John. On one level, as I said before, it does make a difference if the harm was done with intention. But even then, there are two aspects of forgiveness. One is between you and the other person. But one is within you alone, John. And that's the one that applies here.

"Part of the internal aspect is to know that we all have everything within us: love and hate, loyalty and betrayal, kindness and cruelty, aliveness and deadness. If we are willing to know it, John, we all have a peacemaker and even a warmonger within us. We can never be sure what we would be capable of in a given situation. Therefore, we do know that under the same circumstances we might do that very same thing this person has done to us.

"The other part, which has to do only with your inner being, is your personal history. How does your refusing to forgive your daughter relate to your life story? What clues does your dream life give to us about this? I believe your dreams are telling us that what your daughter did at the tender age of five is not really the issue. That she said you had nothing on at all and bit you when you smacked her were innocent, honest, and spontaneous acts of a child. I believe, John, that what you refuse to forgive is that she evoked in you something ancient, something primal, something painful. You feel what she did is unforgivable because what she evoked, you now have to tend to and heal. Your refusing to forgive her, in my opinion, is a defense against doing your own work with those difficult memories."

Absorbing and trusting Aren's hunch, John wondered aloud, "But what could have been evoked from my past?"

"I don't know for sure," Aren answered, "but I suspect it is from your infancy. You told me earlier today that your mother didn't honor your baby body or soul. You knew this, you confided, because she has told you things about your early life and relationship with her, not even realizing what she was telling you about herself.

"You described how she would nurse you when she wanted to, rather than when you were hungry. And you started to gag when you described how she would force her breast into your little mouth, holding it there despite your fear and struggling protests. You even shared with me that you frequently bit her.

"I think this may be what your daughter evoked so long ago. Painful memories you have not worked through. Memories of how your mother felt about you and treated you, and how you came to feel about yourself as a result. Does that resonate for you, John?"

"I'm amazed, Aren. It does feel true. I can't comprehend it all yet. But I do understand what you mean when you say that swearing I would never forgive my daughter was a way to avoid those memories. And maybe a hidden way to say I would never forgive my mother. Or perhaps myself for having bitten her."

"Yes, John. Certainly the first and maybe all three."

"Yikes!" blurted John. "I'd better go tell Beth I forgive her right away."

"It is great progress that you can see this and want to forgive her, John. But remember the process," cautioned Aren. "Take your time to do your own inner work and to find the right timing and way to extend yourself to your daughter."

Beth began having nightmares, again. The same ones she remembered having as a child, an adolescent, and even a young adult. It was dark. She was far, far away from everyone and everything she knew. She was reaching out into black space for her father, screaming, "Daddy! Daddy! I'm sorry. Please forgive me. Please take me back." There was nothing in response. No noise, no movement, nothing visible. Just empty, black space and her own screams, which awakened her night after night.

Beth's roommate and best friend, Mita, came to be with her each time, sitting with her, holding her, rocking her, talking with her. Finally, during one early morning bout, Beth moaned, "He's never gonna forgive me, Mita. He said he wouldn't and he won't. It's useless. It's hopeless."

"Beth," Mita wondered aloud, "as much as you long for your father's forgiveness, perhaps the real issue here is your forgiveness of him. You did nothing to be forgiven for, but his action cries out for forgiveness."

"Hmm." Beth began to come to life from her previously resigned state. "But how do I do that, Mita? He has hurt me so and changed my life beyond comprehension."

"This is not the kind of work we can do alone, Beth. We each need to find someone who can help us where we are blind, as we all are in places. Let's find you a therapist," offered Mita, who had herself worked with a psychotherapist for a number of years. "I'll see if I can get you a couple of solid recommendations."

"Noooooooooo, Mita. I don't want a therapist. You do it with me."

"I can't, Beth. You need someone who is trained to help you through this and has done his or her own journey with forgiveness. There is no quick fix here. It's a process and takes time. If you were preparing a feast, you wouldn't just throw frozen dinners in a microwave, would you? You would give your love and your care to preparations not just on the day of the feast, but for days ahead.

"You don't just write him a letter and say 'I forgive you, Daddy.' You need to work through it at the core of your being. You need slowly to dissolve the defenses you have built to defend against your feelings, and at the same time develop your capacity to feel those feelings. This has been a traumatic experience for you. You need to feel your pain, your anger, your fear — all your feelings. You need to let your own step-by-step experience inform and co-create whatever action you eventually take with him. Your walk through the forgiveness process needs to be about you. In that way *only* will the result be your healing and spiritual development, no matter his response.

"Your heartache and your dreams have brought you to this moment, Beth. Take the next step and trust in the positive possibilities that exist even beyond your imagination."

HERE AND NOW

CHAPTER SEVENTEEN
FORGIVENESS: THE REAL THING

Review . . .

New Age and other leaders teach distortions about forgiveness. Their students have lived by such untruths as, "If you don't forgive, you will not succeed in a relationship; if you forgive, you will achieve inner peace." These axioms can lead to the very problems they are designed to ameliorate.

As a child, Beth told the truth about her father, the Governor. Experiencing her as impudent, he smacked her and raged, "I will never forgive you," then sent her into exile.

The father, John, never forgot the day his little girl publicly exposed and humiliated him.

Years passed. John found Aren, a skilled dream interpreter. Beth found her roommate Mita was an insightful friend. Aren talked with John and Mita with his daughter, teaching them about real forgiveness. They explained that it is impossible to spiritualize away what has affected us in our hearts, cells, and soul substance. Aren and Mita taught that there are two aspects of forgiveness: One is between us and the people we want to forgive; but the more important one is within each of us alone — a co-creation we carry out with Spirit.

Consider . . .

There are so many distortions in our world about forgiveness. There are distortions that threaten and scare people: If you don't forgive, you will not succeed in relationships; if you won't forgive, you will be plagued by guilt the rest of your life; if you can't forgive, you aren't healed; if you fail to forgive, you will not be saved.

There are distortions that seduce, manipulate, and promise something to people: If you forgive, you will achieve inner peace; if you forgive, you will be loved; if you forgive, you can be one with the Divine; if you forgive, it is a sign of emotional maturity.

❖ What other distortions can you add to the list?

❖ Name distortions about forgiveness that you have received, taken in, and lived by. Have you fed these distortions to others?

In this chapter, Aren has helped John, and Mita has helped Beth to understand the true process through which forgiveness emerges.

❖ How have Aren and Mita helped to shed light on your particular experiences with forgiveness?

And Then . . .

John and Beth both did the inner work of forgiveness. Each of them frequently wanted to skip over the rest of the work and contact the other. Fortunately, Aren, as John's therapist, and the therapist Beth found for herself were both wise and firm, cautioning their clients to be patient and thorough with their own work. The results were worth the wait: A healing between John and his daughter so authentic and deep that true forgiveness and reunion were created.

CHAPTER EIGHTEEN

FULFILLMENT

*F*inally, a block away from the castle, a little child's voice was heard saying, "But the Emperor has nothing on at all!" The child's father responded, "Listen to the voice of innocence!" The child's mother responded, "You are so brave, my child, to say the truth when everyone else was silent!" And what the child had said was whispered from one person to another until at last all the people were heard saying, "But the Emperor has nothing on at all!"

The Emperor was drawn to the child as to a magnet. He knelt down on the ground and reached out to her. As she looked at him she saw rivulets of tears streaming down his cheeks. "Don't cry, Your Majesty," she said, reaching out and wiping his tears with her fingers. "We can get you some clothes."

And they smiled at each other and hugged each other. When they parted, they found the town tailor standing beside them. All the while the false weavers had been weaving the false clothes, the real tailor had been sewing the Emperor a suit of clothing, simple but beautiful, and absolutely real! With great love, he handed them to the Emperor, who again wept, this time with joy.

Holding the clothes in his arms, he turned to the townspeople and asked their forgiveness, promising to rebuild himself and his empire in a new, honest, and loving way. The townspeople cheered and cheered.

At this, the little girl jumped up and down laughing and cheering and clapping. Then she felt something on her shoulders. She looked up to see

the smiling tailor and looked down to see that he had placed upon her
shoulders a little cape of golden threads. "Bless you, child. You are a pre-
cious gem. This golden cape is a symbol of the treasure I have always
known you are. Even before today, I knew who you were."

The little girl's smile was so big, it wrapped right around her head and
her heart.

Jewel grew up. She no longer remembered the day when the
Emperor had nothing on at all. She walked through her life feeling
blessed. In the fibers of her soul substance, she felt seen, known, valued,
and loved as her unique and essential Self. This helped her feel supported and appreciated for who she was, but it also made becoming her fullest
Self so much easier.

She stood in awe watching others try to be their unique selves without the experience of being treasured as she had been. She marveled that
in the face of such serious consequences, they could do *at all* what she
did so easily and naturally.

Telling the truth at risk of death. Loving on penalty of humiliation.
Confronting injustice, despite certain imprisonment. Refusing to mask
themselves although the consequence would be shunning.

How her heart opened to these beings who had to work so hard just
to be themselves. She wanted to help. First she needed a deeper sense of
what they were going through. It simply didn't seem right to help them
from her vantage point, so different from their experiences.

So Jewel did some research. She tried to find a location that was most
opposite to the environment in which she grew up. A place where children were violated under the guise of love, even as they screamed "No!"
A place where people went limp in the face of hate, which was really a
disguise for fear. A place where people were accused of being crazy if
they had inspirations for new ways of solving problems or creative ways
for living. A place where people refused to talk about the truth until it
seemed the truth had never existed.

She sought someplace where a young truth-teller might be burned at the stake, while all the adults would stand by. Someplace where an authority would drown a baby to get back at a young child for seeing through him. Someplace where a leader would use a little girl to satisfy his own hungers under the pretense of something sacred, while the whole community, even the women, colluded. Someplace where a whole planet would be mesmerized by popular workshop personalities, allowing and copying their examples of abuse, terrified of confronting their power for fear of retribution.

Jewel looked for a place where people were not conscious of what their sexuality was doing and the impact it was having and had no intention to be conscious. A place where helpers wore masks of kindness to hide their contempt for those who were longing and working to heal themselves.

She searched for a place where people joined the oppressive authorities in an attempt to be safe from them, thereby fueling their abuse of power. A place where people had contempt for the human — the ego, the physical, the heart. A place where people worked their hearts out striving in vain to be recognized, valued, and loved.

Everywhere she traveled outside her hometown, Jewel found some aspect of what she was seeking. But there was one particular land where it seemed all aspects were lived. A sterile, bleak land across the ocean. After days of prayer and preparation within and without, Jewel traveled to this land. Her intention: To know for herself what it was like for those who were not cherished.

She talked to people all across the land, heard stories of horror and expressed her sorrow for their painful lives. Finally, Jewel found herself in a town where a child was being tortured for telling the Commander that he was cruel. This Jewel could not bear. Involuntarily risking her own safety, she moved, as though flying, to the child's side, cut her loose, scooped her up into her arms, and ran . . .

She ran and ran. Who knows for how long? Who knows how she knew the way? Something was guiding her, something greater than her human self. And as she ran, as she carried that child toward safety, she trusted the guidance. Suddenly it was as if a curtain were drawn aside, and Jewel saw that she lived in many times and realms at once. She was aware now of life after life in which she had not been loved for who she was, had not been supported to be the love and truth that she was, had been punished for being her Self. Holding the precious child in her arms, she ran and cried, ran and screamed, sometimes not sure if she was being chased by warriors from other lifetimes or soldiers from the present.

Finally, exhausted and unsure how she would be able to go on, Jewel came to a lake, the child still in her arms. At the edge of the lake waited a boat and a boatwoman, who offered to take them across. Intuiting the trustworthiness of the boatwoman, Jewel accepted. As they traversed the lake, Jewel learned that they were crossing back into safe territory, where the soldiers had no jurisdiction. Where international law, in fact, reigned. Her mind, her heart, and her whole body relaxed. So did her arms, encircling the child. Now she rocked the child gently, singing.

And as she sang her song of safety, Jewel realized she had accomplished her mission: Understanding the plight of those who were not supported to be their real Selves. She had also discovered what it had been like for her to be unloved, unsupported, unvalued in other lifetimes. No wonder she felt such compassion for those in the same situation. No wonder she felt so very blessed in this life.

Her heart wanted to help. Now she knew she could. For she had worked for lifetimes to heal the wound born of not having been loved for her Self. Now Jewel could be who she was, love herself, and allow herself to be loved. Now that she could harvest the fruits of her lifetimes of healing and transformation, so also could she truly, freely, genuinely share them with others.

HERE AND NOW

C H A P T E R E I G H T E E N
FULFILLMENT

Review . . .

Healing the wounds born of being unloved for one's Self is the great
secret to finding true self-love and creating a reality and world where all
are valued for who they are.

In her childhood, Jewel's parents celebrated her truth-telling, and the
Emperor, too, was drawn to her for her truthful, loving ways.

Jewel grew up. She walked through life feeling blessed. In the fibers
of her soul substance, she felt seen, known, valued, and loved as her
unique and essential Self. Jewel wanted to find a place most opposite to
the environment in which she grew up, a place where she could help
those who had to work hard just to be themselves. She found that place
across the ocean and traveled there.

On her journey, she discovered what it had been like for her in
previous lives to be not valued and not supported. Having worked for
lifetimes to heal the wound born of not being loved for her Self, Jewel
knew she was finally ready to help.

Consider . . .

Here, at last, is the truly happy ending: The vision and the
experience of being loved for one's Self.

You may think that such a story could never come true. In fact, this is the reality we are working toward, intending, praying for, and co-creating. This is the reality that is coming into being as we do the inner and outer work of healing power abuse.

Can you dare to believe this?

And Then . . .

Just as in her childhood, Jewel became a healing agent through everything she did — simply by being herself. Her radiant presence carried healing into the world. Her everyday interactions with people brought healing to those she touched and those who witnessed. And the work she did impacted thousands, even millions, with her healing intentions.

EPILOGUE

MY PRAYER FOR OUR WORLD

The right use of our power comes from aligning it with the Divine, by whatever name and in whatever form we know the Divine. It does not come from calling something "the Divine" to serve our own agenda. It does not come from using the Divine as a guise for willful abuse of power nor as a guise for unconscious misuse of power.

Many of us think we know the Divine. But how can we? The Divine is limitless. And even if it weren't, we each approach the Divine from a different direction and make contact with a different aspect of the Divine. Like the old story of the blind people standing around an elephant, each thinking she knows what an elephant is from feeling it, while describing only one part of the elephant — the tail, the trunk, the foot, the ear, the belly.

Even so, many of us think we know the Divine. Yet, if we can transfer early authorities in our lives onto people, we can also transfer early authorities in our lives onto the unknown ultimate authority as though it were a divine entity that looked, thought, felt, spoke, or acted like our mother, our father, our minister...

How have we unconsciously transferred someone from our past onto the Divine?

Ask these questions as prayer:

Who are you, God? I want to know!
What are you, God? I need to know!
Who are you, Goddess? I have to know!

What are you, Goddess? I long to know!
Who are you, God? I pray to know!
What are you, God? Help me know!

Help me clear my images — distortions, misunderstandings, defenses!
Help me heal the wounds . . .
That stand in my way of knowing you, God!
Who you are within my very Self
And who you are in the world outside me.

Ask these questions as exploration:

Who are you, God? I want to know!
Are you like my father who . . .

> *If I come to you, God,*
> *Openly, willingly, innocently,*
> *Will you respond to me as my father did?*

Who are you, Goddess? I want to know!
Are you like my mother who . . .

> *If I come to you, Goddess,*
> *Openly, willingly, innocently,*
> *Will you respond to me as my mother did?*

Who are you, Spirit? I want to know!
Are you like my grandmother who . . .

> *If I come to you, Spirit*
> *Trustingly, wanting to co-create with you,*
> *Will you respond to me as my grandmother did?*

Who are you, O Divine? I want to know!
Are you like my grandfather, who . . .

If I come to you, O Divine,
Trustingly, wanting to co-create with you,
Will you respond to me as my grandfather did?

Who are you, O Source of All That Is?

Are you like . . .
    My brother . . . Why should I trust you?
    My sister . . . Why should I have faith in you?
    My aunt . . . Why should I believe you?
    My uncle . . . Why should I feel safe with you?
    My neighbor . . . Why should I surrender to you?
    My teacher . . . Why should I give myself to you?

Take time to think, feel, and even write responses to the questions. Then transformation can occur.

This work with transference brings to light complex and profound questions for us to ask. Who's to say if the God you say you are aligned with is truly divine? Who's to know if the Goddess to whom you are talking is, in fact, the Divine Feminine? Who's to know if the Buddha from whom you are receiving guidance is beyond a doubt the Divine Buddha?

I have searched and searched to find a way to help us answer these questions. The deepest truth, I believe, is that in this case, the questions are more important than the answers. The questions are themselves a prayer. A prayer that we do not have a static relationship with the Divine, a prayer that our relationship with the Divine is always growing, allowing us to evolve, the relationship to evolve, and the Divine Source to evolve also.

Truly aligning with the Divine calls for continuing our own growth. Truly aligning with the Divine requires doing our own inner work, the work of psyche and soul.

My Prayer

With the cells of my body, I pray for our world:
    May each bruise we have received
    At the hands of someone else's misuse of power,
    Or even our own,
    Call us to healing.
    May each scar we have given others
    Through our own abuse of power
    Call us to rebirth.
    May the Call be so loud
    We cannot ignore it.

With my heart, I pray for our world:
    May we be compelled,
    Person by person,
    To walk toward the right use of power,
    Compelled by our own free will,
    Called by the unstoppable development of our souls,
    Guided by the magnificent longing in our spirits.

With my soul, I pray for our world:
    May the spiritual understanding of
    'The poison is the medicine,'
    Which I have known to be true,
    Be true in this time.
    May this era of epidemic
    Misuse and abuse of power
    In every arena of life
    Serve as an effective remedy,
    Leading us to heal and live the right use of power.

With my spirit I pray for our world:
    May each one of us become
    The very essence of the right use of power.

                    May This Come To Be . . .

GLOSSARY

These definitions are based on the author's professional experience, rather than the dictionary, to enhance understanding of the book.

Abuse — Improper treatment or use; misuse; to hurt or injure physically, emotionally, or spiritually; a misuse of our natural powers.

Abuse Dynamic — A pattern of interactions in which at least one person is misusing his or her power.

Abuse of Power — Improper treatment or misuse of power, especially by someone in a position of authority.

Collective Consciousness — A body of accumulated awareness created by the conscious and unconscious psyches of individuals.

Conscious — Aware; having present knowledge or perception of oneself, one's thoughts, feelings, and actions, alone or in relation to one's surroundings.

Core Belief — A person's basic view of reality, deeply rooted in the unconscious; it may be accurate or terribly distorted.

Counter-transference — A therapist's conscious or unconscious emotional reaction and/or behavior toward the client. (See transference.)

Depth Psychotherapy — Exploration of the hidden or repressed Self to discover the roots of current behaviors resulting from early childhood experiences with the objective of healing, growth, and transformation.

Defense — Psychological means or mechanisms often unconscious, even involuntary, originally meant to protect us in the face of feelings so intense we believe they are unbearable.

Denial — Refusal to realize or admit the truth of existing circumstances.

Duality — Two opposing principles; the tendency to create black and white opposites: dark and light, love and hate, good and evil.

Dynamics — A pattern of conscious and/or unconscious interactions between people.

Early Decision — A conscious or unconscious decision made in childhood — about oneself, others, and life — that drives a person's life choices.

Ego — The part of human personality experienced as the "self" or "I."

Erotic Transference — Experiencing romantic and sexual thoughts and feelings because of those same feelings in childhood.

Goddess — Female creator, mother of the universe; feminine essence; source of life, holding life sacred and helping life unfold organically.

Grief — Mental, emotional, physical, spiritual suffering associated with loss.

Group Consciousness — See Collective Consciousness.

Group Therapy — A group of individuals, under the guidance of a trained therapist, meeting together for self-exploration and healing.

Intuition — Awareness or knowing without conscious use of reasoning; an inner knowing.

Jungian — Refers to a theoretical psychoanalytic system based on the theories of Carl Jung.

Maze — An inner vicious cycle created by the interplay of our experiences and early decisions.

Mystery — The mystical unfolding and interplay of life events, comprehended not by intellect or even the senses, but rather by the soul, through our connection with the Divine Source; another name for the Divine.

Poison Is the Medicine — The discomfort of the symptom leads a person to heal the root cause of that symptom. In this case, the discomfort of the symptom is the poison.

Polar Opposites — Direct opposites such as yes/no, peace/violence, good/bad, dark/light.

Premature Transcendence — Attempting to rise above a feeling, pain, or wound before facing and working through it.

Psyche — The integration of the human self and soul.

Psychoanalyst — A professional trained in the branch of mental health known as psychoanalysis.

Psychotherapy — The treatment and/or healing of mental or emotional struggles by working with a professional trained in the study of the psyche.

Repression — The burying of frightening wishes, thoughts, feelings, or experiences.

Resistance — Inner opposition; refusal to face oneself, reality, the truth.

Right Action — Action that is principled.

Ritual — A ceremony.

self — The human self — mind, body, and heart. The concept of self is similar to the concept of ego. Many people want to transcend it, repress it, shame it into hiding — essentially get rid of it. The intention is to help the self grow into its fullness, maturity, ripeness, abundant harvest; to recognize and honor that each time a part of the self grows into fullness it is ready to surrender itself to union with the Self. (See Chapter Ten — "Bye-Bye, Ego")

Self — The spirit Self; the divine essence. Each of us has a unique divine essence that we are here to be, to give, and to bring to fruition. It is the essential nature of who we are — undistorted, undiluted, undefended, and freed into full living by the work of consciousness, growth, healing, and transformation.

Shadow — A part of the unconscious with both positive and negative traits, which the conscious self tends to ignore or reject.

Spirit — A person's vital life force, his or her unique essence.

Spiritual Counselor — One who guides an individual in matters of the spirit, often on an inward journey to discover the spiritual Self.

Spiritual Midwife — One who assists in the birthing and journey of another's soul; one who helps a person bring his or her essence into matter.

Spiritual Therapist — A psychotherapist who embraces and integrates spirituality, helps clients discover and develop their connection with the Divine.

Spiritual Truth — A fundamental, authentic reality grounded in the essence of the life force.

Split — To separate parts of self; for example, ignoring the perceived "negative side" or "lower self" and focusing only on the positive parts of the Self. Dividing or separating layers of the Self creates a split.

Tantra — Sacred spiritual practice using sexual experience to connect with the Divine.

Therapeutic — Tending to cure or restore to health and wholeness.

Transference — The unconscious transfer or redirection of feelings and attitudes originally associated with important childhood figures onto people or situations in current life.

Unconscious — Feelings and content of the self that are not ordinarily available to awareness.

THE AUTHOR

Judith Barr is passionate about her desire to help heal and transform the planet and is committed to making a difference one-by-one and on a global scale. She brings to her practice a tapestry of natural gifts interwoven with her life experience and professional skills — combining her deep roots in psychotherapy with her own growing-edge spiritual midwifery, the practice of serving as midwife to the birthing and journey of another's soul.

Judith practices in Brookfield, Connecticut. Her background includes private practice as a depth psychotherapist since 1975, a Master of Science degree in Counseling, and licensure as a Mental Health Counselor. She has published an audio series, *The Spoken Word on Behalf of the Feminine*, and more than two dozen articles for both professionals and the general public. Judith offers her healing expertise in an array of formats, including working with individuals, groups, workshops, and consultations. In addition to this she offers training and supervision programs for healing arts professionals.

Her work with power and the birth of this book inspire her to explore beyond her imagination ... how she can be of further service in our world. Judith invites you to explore and co-create ways in your life to grow, deepen, and transform beyond *your* imagination.

Judith Barr
P.O. Box 603, Brookfield, CT 06804
www.PowerAbusedPowerHealed.com

MORE PRAISE FOR
POWER ABUSED, POWER HEALED

"Judith Barr, who well knows the healing power of story, has compiled an inspirational book of stories, including provocative questions, on the misuse of power. This is a touching, inspirational and prayer-filled book."

— **Pamela D. Blair, Ph.D., psychotherapist, spiritual counselor, and author of** *The Next Fifty Years: A Guide for Women at Midlife & Beyond*

"Power itself is not inherently bad; it is more an issue of how we use power. Too often, in our daily encounters, we are confronted with power-over in its many guises, from big-brother government to parental dominance to therapist authority.

"In *Power Abused, Power Healed,* Judith Barr helps us see, move through, and heal from power-over and offers us an alternative, power-from-within. This use of power allows us to mend the tattered hoop of life."

— **Pam Montgomery, herbalist and author of** *Partner Earth: A Spiritual Ecology*

"Judith Barr speaks with the voice of our common consciousness. Her realization that we are all part of one humanity gives her the insight to delve into the issue of power and abuse.

"This book is a useful tool to help us all recognize how we are affected by the misuse of power. With this awareness we can take responsibility as a parent, therapist, business person, educator, or clergy to use the power of these positions, not for personal gain but for the benefit of all humanity."

— **Katherine Lindseth, Taoist minister and director, Tao Healing Arts Society of New York**

"Judith writes with wisdom, compassion, and commitment, providing an understanding of how and why people misuse and abuse power. She uncovers the many facets of healing the root cause of power abuse and offers a hopeful vision for human evolution as we align the right use of our power with our higher selves."

— **Jackie Hart, licensed massage therapist**